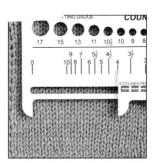

I've been so fortunate to have found some amazing teachers and designers who have so generously provided their expertise in the field of knitting finishing techniques. Thanks to their vast knowledge and ability to explain the methods in an easy-to-understand way, you'll find that many of the questions that have left you stumped in the past will finally be answered.

The methods in *The Perfect Finish* are presented in an easy-to-grasp format, with step-by-step photos to help you along the way. On the pages that follow, you'll see that we start things off with *The Basics*, where we begin with a rundown of the

most important *Tools & Equipment* you'll need before you get working. Then, we present a comprehensive chapter on *Making the Gauge Swatch*, and why it's a crucial component in the preparation process. We then move on to *Preplanning With Finishing in Mind*. You will find yourself referring back to this chapter every time you plan a project. Then, we've arranged the succeeding chapters so that you can quickly find specific techniques necessary for your given project. You'll find a generous range of finishing techniques such as *Creating The Perfect Pocket, The ABCs of Buttonholes* and *Enticing Embellishments*.

The Perfect Finish will become one of those go-to standbys in your knitting library, and perhaps it may even have those handy little sticky notes randomly placed about for future reference. It's my hope that you'll find this book to be an invaluable resource for years to come, and that you'll take joy in the finishing process of all of your knitted creations!

Kara Gott Warner

Contents

The Basics

Finishing 101

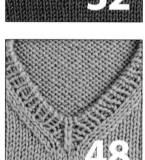

The Perfect Finish™

Edited by Kara Gott Warner

HOUSE of
WHITE
BIRCHES

PUBLISHERS
SINCE 1947

The Perfect Finish™

EDITOR Kara Gott Warner
ART DIRECTOR Brad Snow
PUBLISHING SERVICES DIRECTOR Brenda Gallmeyer

MANAGING EDITOR Barb Sprunger
ASSISTANT ART DIRECTOR Nick Pierce
COPY SUPERVISOR Michelle Beck
COPY EDITOR Emily Carter, Amanda Scheerer
TECHNICAL EDITOR Charlotte Quiggle
TECHNICAL ARTIST Nicole Gage, Pam Gregory

GRAPHIC ARTS SUPERVISOR Erin Augsburger
GRAPHIC ARTISTS Jessi Butler, Minette Collins Smith
PRODUCTION ASSISTANTS Marj Morgan, Judy Neuenschwander

PHOTOGRAPHY SUPERVISOR Tammy Christian
PHOTOGRAPHY Matthew Owen
PHOTO STYLISTS Tammy Liechty, Tammy Steiner

Printed in China
First Printing: 2010
Library of Congress Number: 2001012345
Hardcover ISBN: 978-1-59217-284-9
Softcover ISBN: 978-1-59217-285-6

RETAIL STORES: If you would like to carry this book or any other
DRG publications, visit DRGwholesale.com

Every effort has been made to ensure that the instructions in
this publication are complete and accurate. We cannot, however,
take responsibility for human error, typographical mistakes or
variations in individual work. Please visit AnniesCustomerCare.com
to check for pattern updates.

DRGbooks.com

1 2 3 4 5 6 7 8 9

Finishing Details: "The Extras"

Bonus Project Gallery

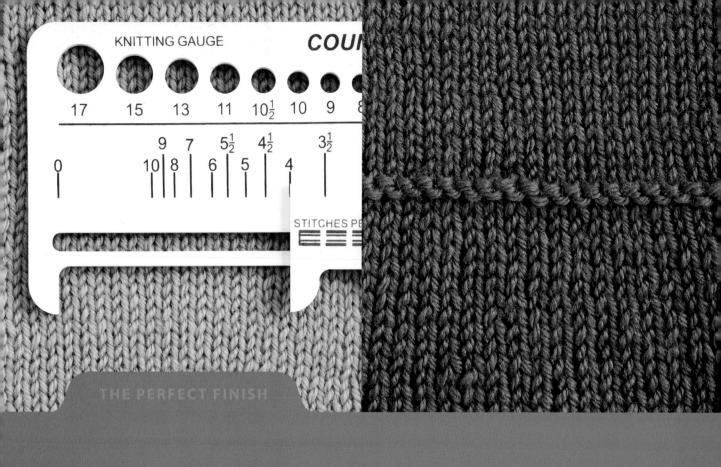

The Basics

Here's where you'll find the nuts-and-bolts basics to garment finishing. It's nice to jump in and get working, but taking some time before you begin ensures that your project will be a success.

Tools & Equipment

If you stock your tool kit with these essentials, you'll always be prepared for every finishing challenge! Since many of these items are small, it's a good idea to keep all your odds and ends in a small, portable case so everything is conveniently in one place.

Knitting Needles

When choosing your needles, it's best to work with what feels most comfortable to you. The most common kinds of needles are made from plastic, metal, wood or bamboo. Circular needles are a must for working in the round; however, they can also be used for back and forth projects for comfort and ease, especially with large projects. Interchangeable circular needle sets are a life saver, because all your needles are organized in one neat case. Double-point needles are good to have handy in order to make I-cords, hats or other small areas of a project where a circular needle just won't cut it.

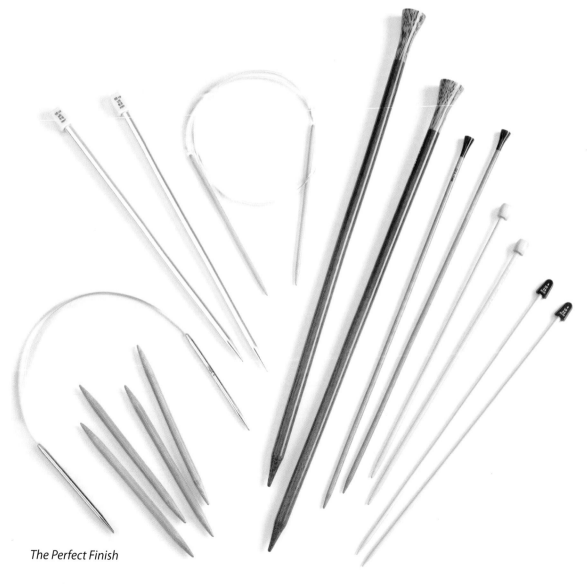

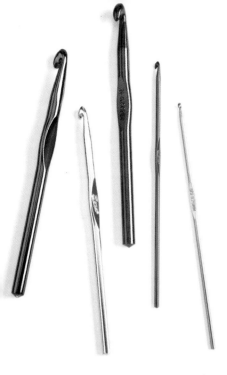

Stitch Holders ▼

These are perfect companions when working a garment. Many times you may need to place your sleeves onto stitch holders in order to sew to an armhole later, or a pattern may require working parts of the neck separately, requiring several small stitch holders. You can even use your own "homemade" stitch holder by having spare bits of waste yarn to slip your live stitches onto for working later.

Row Counters ▲

When working a complicated pattern, it's nice to have counters do the work for you so you don't forget where you left off.

Crochet Hooks ▲

These are indispensable for a variety of reasons: to pick up a dropped stitch, to work a decorative crochet edge or to join pieces of your knitting together instead of sewing.

Point Protectors ▼

These are great for storing away your projects if they are kept on the needle, and to also keep your work from falling off.

Tapestry Needles ▲

These come in various sizes from blunt to fine-point to curved. It's always good to have a variety of sizes and shapes on hand. A straight tapestry needle is good for weaving in loose threads, and a curved tapestry needle is used specifically for seaming in mattress stitch.

Cable Needles ▲

These are designed to work cables; they are small, angular needles with a point on either end. The angular shape makes it easy to slip on a stitch or two and to hold them easily out of the way.

Pins ▼

Small straight pins and dressmaker's pins are good for pinning areas of your garment before seaming or for trying on before assembly. Dressmaker's pins are probably the best choice because they are much larger and keep your pieces securely in place. Non-rusting stainless steel pins are essential for blocking. Safety pins have a variety of uses, too. For example, they can be a real life saver for pinning a sleeve cap into an armhole.

Markers ▲

Markers are the perfect solution for plotting increases and decreases, and to mark check points in a stitch repeat. Don't leave home without them!

Bobbins ▼

These are designed for working patterns where several colors are called for on the same row. They allow you to wind small bits of yarn onto each bobbin making it easier to work.

Tape Measure and Ruler ▼

You should always have a ruler available to measure your gauge swatch or your project as you knit it. It's much more reliable than a tape measure since a tape measure can stretch over time. Having a tape measure is essential for taking body measurements and measuring large areas of your work. Be sure to replace your tape measure every few years, or more often, if it is used frequently.

Scissors ▲

Instead of searching for those big clunky scissors, keep small sharp scissors handy in your finishing essentials arsenal.

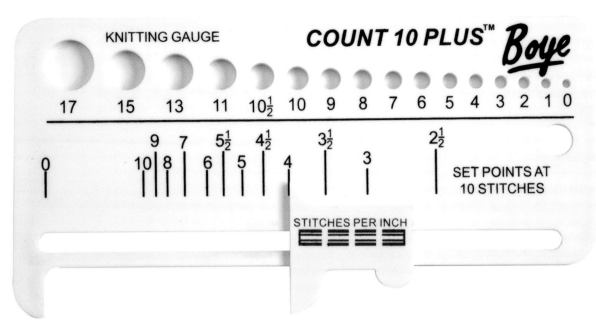

Needle Gauge ⋀

A needle gauge is indispensable for a few reasons. Many circular needles or older straight needles may not have the sizes marked on them. A needle gauge takes away the mystery by sizing your needle. Most needle gauges also have a built-in ruler, making them a handy measuring tool as well.

Other Essentials:

Page Protectors

These are useful for protecting your pattern while working and if you travel with your knitting. You can place your sticky notes on them, and even use a dry-erase pen to make notes.

Sticky Notes

These are indispensable for remembering where you last left off on a pattern, or to take important notes.

Calculator

For some added peace of mind, it's a good idea to have a calculator handy to help you double check stitch or row counts, or parts of a pattern repeat.

Graph paper

Graph paper is necessary if you want to chart a written-out stitch pattern, or if you would like to plan your own design. Graph paper can also be a great visual tool if you want to redraw parts of your schematics to help make better sense of them.

Pencils

Mechanical pencils are good to have in your case because you don't have to worry about sharpening them, and they are better than pens in case you need to revise your notes.

HANDY TOOL TIP

When it comes to storing away and organizing your tools and equipment, here are a few helpful ideas:

1. Store your circular needles in a CD case, and place a sticky note on the inside of each sleeve, showing which size needle is in each.

2. A bead caddy is the perfect solution to store away pins, stitch markers, stitch holders and other small items in your arsenal.

3. Make a mini travel kit from an old make-up case: toss in a sticky note pad, a small scissor, pins and a tape measure.

Making the Gauge Swatch

By Jodi Lewanda

Working a gauge swatch is a crucial first step in creating a well-fitting sweater.

A gauge (or tension) swatch is a sample of your knitting created with the yarn, needle size and pattern stitch that you will be using to work your project. It is used to ensure that your fabric will have the same number of stitches and rows per inch as the sample in the pattern. If you don't achieve the specified gauge when you knit your piece, the size and texture of the project will be different from what the designer intended. This step in the knitting process is crucial to determine whether your combination of yarn, needle size and type and the way you control the yarn as you knit will create the desired result—a well-fitting sweater!

When choosing yarn, it's a good idea to get familiar with the CYCA symbols as shown in Figure 1. Most yarn companies provide this information on their yarn labels. They show the stockinette stitch gauge that they recommend for the yarn by showing the number of stitches and rows that will equal 4 inches; this will help you determine whether the yarn is suitable for your chosen project, especially if you are substituting a different yarn for the one given in the pattern.

Making Your Gauge Swatch

Using the same yarn you plan to use for your project (including the same color, because different colors of the same yarn may have slightly different properties) and the suggested needle size, cast on at least 4 inches of stitches (6 inches is better!), plus at least 2 extra stitches on each end. Since edge stitches worked in stockinette stitch tend to stretch or curl, many knitters like to work those stitches in garter stitch so that they lie flat—you won't be measuring at the edges, so they won't affect your measurements. The larger you make your swatch, the more accurate your stitch and row count measurements will be because you will be able to measure several points on the swatch and average the resulting stitch or row counts.

Use the needle type intended to complete the project because different materials (metal, plastic, wood) have different surfaces which can affect the size of the stitch.

Most often, the gauge is given in stockinette stitch for a 4-inch square. However, if the gauge is given over a pattern stitch, cast on enough stitches for 2 complete repeats of the pattern (plus edge stitches) or 4–6 inches, whichever is greater. Work until the swatch measures at least 4½ inches high, and then bind off very loosely or put the stitches on waste yarn—you don't want the top edge to be tight or pull in.

Gauge Swatches for Circular Knitting

If you are going to work your garment in the round, your swatch should not be worked back and forth. Many knitters tension their yarn differently when purling and

 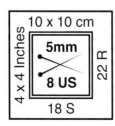 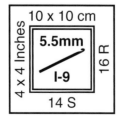 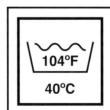 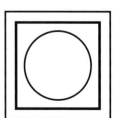

Fig. 1

this will affect the gauge of fabric worked in the round because it tends to have much less purling (in fact, there's none if the fabric is stockinette stitch). There are two easy methods for working an in-the-round gauge swatch while still working flat; both require that you always work with the right side of the fabric facing you. The first method requires that you cut the yarn when you get to the end of the row, slide the swatch back to the end of the needle, and then re-attach the yarn and knit the next row with the right side facing. The downside of this method is that you will not be able to re-use the yarn if necessary. The other option is to work the swatch without cutting the yarn, but instead carrying it very loosely behind the needle in a big loop, and then starting the next row with the right side facing you.

If you will be working your garment in the round to the underarms, then splitting it for front and back and working them back and forth, work two gauge swatches—one "flat" swatch and one "circular" swatch. You may need to change needle sizes when working the different sections of the sweater in order to remain on gauge.

Measuring Your Stitches

Once it's completed, wash and block your gauge swatch the way you intend to wash and block the finished garment (refer to Blocking Fundamentals, page 32 for more information). The reason for washing the swatch is that many yarns bloom, stretch or contract after being washed, and that can affect the size of your stitches. Do not stretch the drying swatch unless instructed to do so. When the swatch is completely

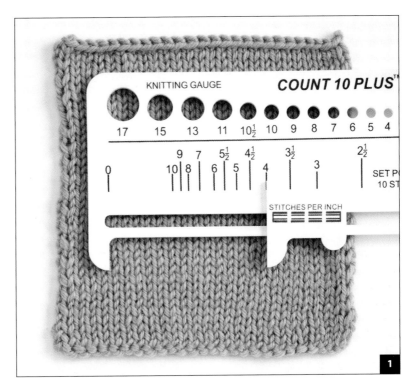

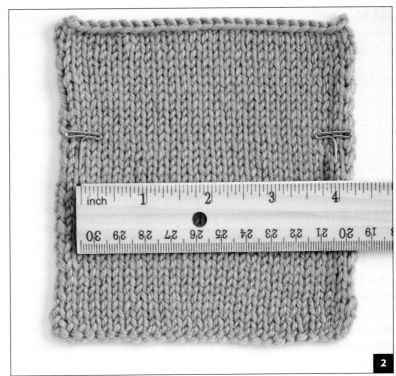

dry, lay it on a flat surface and measure horizontally; it's better to measure with a ruler because a tape measure can stretch over time. As shown in Photo 1, a gauge tool is another helpful method for

taking your measurement. Place pins 4 inches apart, as shown in Photo 2, and then count the number of stitches between the pins to determine your stitch gauge. A very careful count is important here (half-stitches count!) to ensure correct gauge and to guarantee a perfect fit. Now, measure in two more places and average the three for best accuracy.

Row Gauge

Don't forget row gauge—it is also very important, especially when working raglan or side-to-side garments. As shown in Photo 3, measure the same swatch vertically with the same tool you used for the horizontal measurement and place pins. Count the number of rows between pins to determine row count. If it's not the row count called for in the pattern, your shaped pieces (such as sleeve caps) may be too short or too long, and you will have to compensate by working more or fewer rows if you have already achieved the correct stitch gauge.

Weighted Gauge Swatches

Garments made from inelastic fibers (superwash wool, alpaca, cotton or silk) will often stretch when worn; so will many large garments, like coats, merely because of their weight. They tend to gradually become narrower and longer. You want to know this ahead of time so that you can plan for the stretching. The best way to do this is by taking an extra step before measuring your gauge. After your washed swatch is dry, measure the gauge swatch flat as indicated above. Then take a "weighted gauge" as follows: pin the swatch to a hanger, run a knitting needle through the bottom edge, then hang a skein of yarn from that needle. Let it hang for a day (or longer), then measure the gauge on the swatch *while it's hanging*. Take note of both the flat gauge and the weighted

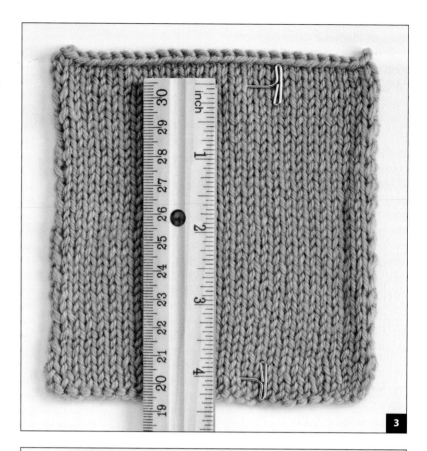

3

4

gauge. If the weighted gauge has stretched, you will want to work proportionally fewer rows in your actual garment.

Changing Needle Sizes

Changing the needle size to obtain the correct gauge is essential. Gauge is all-important—there is no need to knit with the needle size given in the pattern because everyone knits differently. The needle size suggested in the pattern is the size that the designer used to achieve gauge, but your stitches may be tighter or looser than the designer's stitches.

As illustrated in Photo 4, if after measuring your gauge swatch, you find that you are getting more stitches or rows in 4 inches than specified in the pattern, your stitches are too small; you must change to a larger needle size and knit another swatch.

If there are too few stitches in your 4-inch square, as Photo 5 illustrates, your stitches are too large; change to a smaller needle size, and re-work and re-measure your swatch.

Sometimes using a needle of the same size, but of a different material (metal vs. wood) will be enough of a change to achieve the correct gauge.

If you don't know the recommended needle size for your yarn, you should make one swatch using different needle sizes. If you refer to Photo 6, you will see that each needle-size section should be separated by a row of purl stitches on the knitted side or some other dividing mark. This is a great way to compare the different fabrics that you can get from the same yarn just by changing gauge.

5

6

Measuring Ribbing

Measuring the gauge of an elastic fabric, such as ribbing, can be a little tricky. Most patterns will indicate that the ribbed gauge should be taken over fabric that is either slightly stretched or left unstretched. The measuring and pinning technique previously described should be used for ribs. Two important points to remember when measuring ribbing are to take care not to flatten the ribbing and not to forget to count the background stitches—the purl stitches between the knit stitches. Photo 7 demonstrates how to measure the swatch with the ribbing stretched, and Photo 8, unstretched.

Final Thoughts

Make sure to check your gauge periodically as you work through your project, about every 6 inches or so. Occasionally, as we become more familiar with a yarn, needles and/or a stitch pattern, we relax and loosen our tension. ■

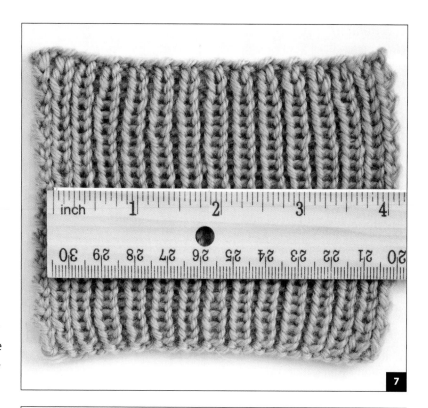

Preplanning With Finishing in Mind

By Kate Atherley

It's so exciting to jump right into a new project, but taking the time to plan each step will guarantee a perfect finish!

A little bit of planning before you start knitting can significantly ease the finishing burden for any project—and it's sure to make your finished garment look and wear better.

Materials and Equipment

Check the materials and equipment list to make sure you have everything you need. You don't want to be caught without that all-important cable needle (or a suitable substitute) when your local yarn shop is closed.

And don't forget about the additional notions that might be required—yarn needles for sewing, stitch holders, buttons, a good blunt-end yarn needle and a selection of safety pins. The pattern doesn't always mention them, but trust me, if there are seams to be sewn, you'll need a yarn needle and safety pins.

Read Ahead

Take time to read through the pattern before you begin any project in order to make sure you have all the required skills and to see what adjustments can be made to make the finishing easier.

Check to see whether there are any techniques or stitches you're not familiar with. For example, if a pattern calls for a special cast-on or bind-off, look it up and practice it if it's new to you. Don't stress too much about following every line of the instructions; some of them won't make sense until you get there. For example, it can be hard to visualize which is the right side of a piece until you have it in your hands. The idea is to be prepared for things like simultaneous shaping of armholes and necklines, changes in pattern stitches, etc. And pay particular attention to the order in which you knit the garment and the finishing instructions.

A typical garment can be finished in stages; you don't need to wait until the end. Most often, you knit the back and front (or fronts, if it's a cardigan) of the garment first. For all but raglan-sleeve designs, you can sew the front and back pieces together as soon as they're blocked and even work the neckline treatment. There's no need to wait until the sleeves are ready before you start assembling. This not only breaks up the finishing effort, but can provide encouragement. Personally, I get a great sense of achievement from seeing the pieces come

together—it feels so much closer to a completed garment if I can try it on! And being able to try a sweater on helps with fitting. Once you know where the shoulder line falls, you can measure to see if you need to make adjustments to the sleeve length.

Check Your Gauge

Just do it! It will save a lot of grief in the end. It's the only way to ensure your garment will turn out to be the size you're expecting. If you're not matching the specified gauge, do change your needles.

Swatching also gives you a sense of what the yarn is like to work with. In addition to allowing you to determine what the right needle size is, it will help you decide if a particular type of needle is better. For a slippery yarn, you might prefer working with wooden or bamboo needles; for a textured or sticky yarn, metal needles can be better. You will also get familiar with the stitch pattern while you work the swatch.

Manage Your Tails

When you're casting on, if you leave a long tail of 12 inches, you can use it for sewing seams later. (Tie tails into a slip knot as you're working, so you don't accidentally use one instead of the working yarn!)

If you're working back and forth, always change yarns at the beginning or end of a row—it looks neater, and you'll be able to weave the ends into the seams. And again, leave a long tail in case you need it for seaming.

There are two exceptions to this rule: If the yarn you're knitting with is not appropriate for seaming—refer to the seaming chapter for more on this—or if you plan to take the garment apart again. It's much easier to take apart a garment if you've used separate lengths of yarn for seaming. If you don't plan to use the tails for seaming, then a 6-inch tail will suffice.

Eliminating Seams

You can eliminate some of the seams entirely by working pieces in the round, rather than flat. Sleeves in particular are easy to convert, which can save a lot of seaming effort.

You can also work the body pieces together, up to the underarms, to avoid side seams. With a cardigan, you'll work back and forth; for a pullover, you'll work in the round. For smaller garments, and especially for kids' clothes, it's a great time saver. Working the body in one piece is not recommended for every garment, however. A larger garment, or one worked in a heavy non-elastic yarn, like alpaca or thick cotton, needs side seams for structure to reduce the risk of stretching and sagging.

If you are going to do this, it's always a good idea to check your gauge to make sure you're getting

the same in the round as flat—you may need to use different size needles for working in the round. You don't want the parts worked in the round to have a different gauge from those worked back and forth.

Edges

If you're going to be picking up stitches along a horizontal edge—the back of the neck, for example—bind off loosely and evenly.

If your project has a garter stitch edge with no additional band or seaming required, work a chain selvage by slipping the first stitch—it makes for a very neat, finished edge.

If you're going to be seaming or picking up stitches along an edge, don't slip the first stitch of the row. Some knitters will tell you it makes it easier to sew the seams. It actually doesn't. Not only is seaming or picking up in chain (slipped stitch) selvages messy—the holes may be visible—but you also cut the number of locations for picking up stitches in half. In general, stockinette stitch selvage stitches are best for edges that will be seamed using mattress stitch or will be used for picked-up bands.

Placing Your Increases and Decreases

Correct placement of increases and decreases can make your project much easier to sew.

No matter how simple a garment, there are usually some increases and decreases to work for shaping, at least on the sleeve and neckline. For a design with a set-in sleeve, decreases are necessary to shape both the armhole on the body and the sleeve cap.

Smart placement of increases and decreases can make your seaming much easier; instead of working them right at the beginning or end of the row, do them 1 or 2 stitches in from the edge.

For example, if a pattern said to decrease 1 stitch at both ends of right side rows, you might be inclined to work your favorite decrease at the very beginning and end of row, e.g. k2tog, knit to last 2 sts, k2tog. Don't! This will produce an uneven edge with no selvage stitches, making it much more difficult to sew into. For stockinette stitch fabric, it's best to use mirrored decreases.

Try this instead: K1 (or 2), ssk, knit to last 3 (or 4) sts, k2tog, k1 (or 2).

Mirrored decreases are less important if you're working in garter stitch because the decreases aren't as visible.

A commonly used increase for sleeves is kfb (knit in the front and back of the stitch). Although easy to work, it creates a little bump in your row, and if worked on the first or last stitch of a row, it creates an uneven edge. Instead, use mirrored lifted or M1 increases, and work them 1 or 2 stitches in from the edge, e.g., k2, increase

---

EDGING TIP

You may wonder why binding off is required if you're going to be picking up stitches along that edge later. The bind-off is there for structure, to prevent stretching and sagging.

(leaning right), knit to last 2 stitches, increase (leaning left), k2.

In either case, what you'll get is a nice, even straight edge that is much easier to sew.

Short Row Shoulder Shaping

Adding short rows is a more advanced adaptation, but one that can reduce the seaming and create a better-looking result.

A tailored, fitted garment with a set-in sleeve will often have a sloped shoulder line. Some patterns call for binding off the shoulder stitches in two or three stages. Instead of working these as bind-offs, refer to The Art of Short Rows, page 106. That way all shoulder stitches can be kept live, and front and back shoulders can be joined using 3-needle bind-off—one more seam eliminated!

Allow Yourself the Time

Remember that finishing does take time; before you put them together, you'll need to wash or block the pieces and wait for them to dry. And you'll need to set aside

a few hours for the actual process of seaming and weaving in ends.

If you're working to a deadline—and who hasn't, when making holiday gifts, or creating a garment for a special event—make sure you complete the knitting two or three days before you need to wear (or gift-wrap) the project.

You can get a head start by finishing as you go, but there will always be some final work to do: plan ahead so you have the time.

A rushed finishing job shows. No matter how good your knitting, poor finishing can ruin the look of the completed project.

Don't Shy Away From Seaming

Of course, there is a temptation to choose only seamless garments in an attempt to reduce (or entirely eliminate) the finishing work.

Seamless knitting makes perfect sense for many types of garments—socks, for example. A seam would rub against your foot. But a fitted or shaped garment benefits enormously from seams. The seams create shape and structure.

A pieced garment allows more flexibility in shapes, styles and fit; if you go with only one-piece garments, you're depriving yourself of some really great garments.

And the seams themselves have benefits: As mentioned, they provide structure and help reduce sagging and stretching. They're also a great place to hide your yarn tails.

And seams allow you to hide the ends of your rows, too. No matter how good a knitter you are, the first and last stitch of a row can be a bit awkward—it's because you work the same stitch twice in succession, and as a result, the stitch tends to twist and wobble a little. Seaming allows you to hide those inconsistent looking stitches.

Enjoy the Process

The more prepared you are in the beginning, the smoother the finishing process will go. Mapping out your plan of action ahead of time will guarantee success in the end. Just as a rushed finishing job can make a mess of a beautifully knitted garment, a careful finishing job can take a project from good to great. ■

Finishing 101

In this chapter, a select group of teachers and designers offer their knowledge on a variety of finishing methods. If you're looking for the best way to block your cabled cardigan, then Blocking Fundamentals with Jennifer Hagan will show you how. If inserting a zipper has you in a quandary, then Leslye Solomon will solve your dilemma in Wonderful World of Working With Zippers.

Special Cast-On & Bind-Off Methods

By Kate Atherley

Choosing just the right cast-on or bind-off method, can make your design shine!

Every knitter knows at least one cast-on and bind-off, but there are a wide variety of methods for doing each. Some are best suited to specific uses; others are good for general use. These are just a few of the many options.

There are two main considerations to bear in mind: how you want the edge to look and how you want it to behave. You will want a stretchy bind-off for sections that need to stretch, but a firm cast-on where you don't want the edge to flare. For example, lace pieces and the tops of top-down socks need elastic cast-ons, while cables need firm cast-ons. The cuffs of toe-up socks and the neck of a turtleneck pullover need stretchy bind-offs.

Expert Tips

1. With any cast-on or bind-off, leave at least a 6-inch tail. These ends are long enough to weave in neatly.

2. Longer tails can be used for seaming, as long as the yarn itself is suitable. See the chapter on seaming (page 38) for more information.

3. If you have to cast on a lot of stitches, place a safety pin or marker after every 20 stitches to help you keep count.

4. Double and triple check the number of cast-on stitches before you start working. There's nothing worse than finding out you're short a stitch halfway through your piece.

Long Tailed (or Double) Cast-On

This is a terrific all-purpose cast-on, providing a firm but still stretchy edge. The resulting edge looks very similar to a standard bind-off.

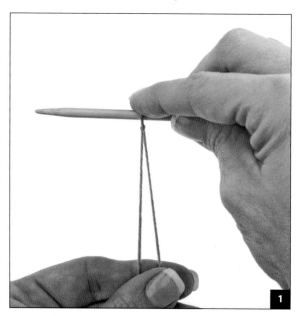

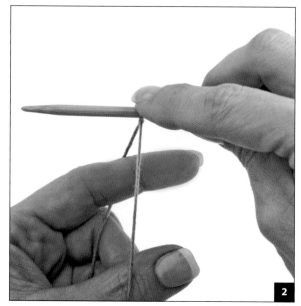

Referring to Photos 1-7, make a slip knot a good distance up the yarn, leaving a long tail. Put the slip knot on needle and hold the needle in your right hand.

Step 1: Make a fist with your left hand around the two strands of yarn and pull down to get some tension as shown in Photo 1.

Step 2: Separate the two strands with your thumb and forefinger spread apart as shown in Photo 2, and tilt your palm up. The yarn leading to the ball should be over your forefinger. The point of the needle should be positioned between your outstretched thumb and forefinger as shown in Photo 3.

Step 3: With the needle, swoop over and pick up the thread on the far side of your thumb as shown in Photo 4.

Step 4: Now, swoop over and pick up the thread on the near side of your forefinger as shown in Photo 5.

Step 5: Bring the needle back toward you, through the loop of yarn that's around your thumb as shown in Photo 6.

Step 6: Drop the yarn, pull the stitch snugly—but not tightly—around the needle as shown in Photo 7 on page 24.

Repeat Steps 1–6. As you get more proficient, you'll be able to let the yarn ends flow through your fingers, and you won't need to reposition them every time.

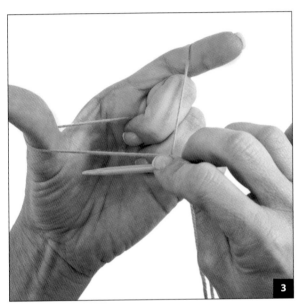

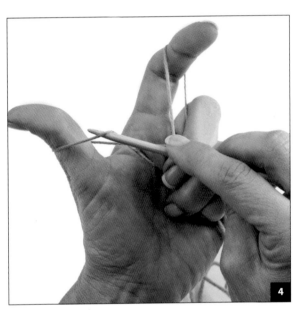

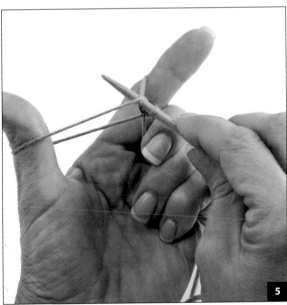

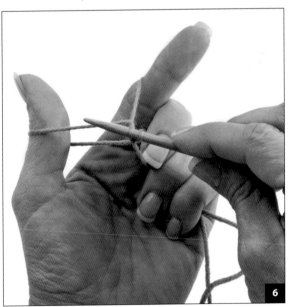

Backwards Loop Cast-On

This is the first cast-on that many knitters learn. It's very easy to do, but the first row is a little challenging to work. It's a handy one to use if you need to cast on stitches at the beginning or end of a row.

Following the steps shown in Photos 8–10; start by making a slip knot, leaving a 6-inch tail. Put the slip knot on the needle and hold the needle in your right hand.

Step 1: Pick up the working yarn with your left hand, to create a loop as demonstrated in Photo 8,

Step 2: Twist the loop around a half turn to the right, until it crosses over itself as in Photo 9.

Step 3: Put the loop on the needle and pull the working yarn to tighten as shown in Photo 10.

Repeat Steps 1–3.

7

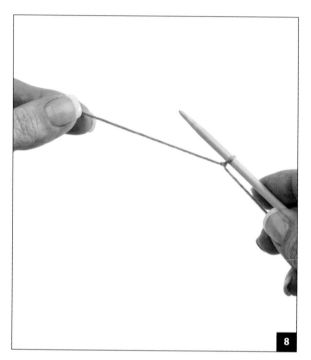

8

9

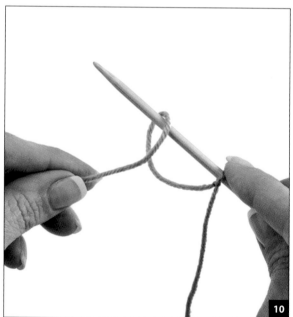

10

Cable Cast-On

This cast-on is nice and firm; it's also a good choice for adding stitches at either end of a row or in the middle of a row, such as for a horizontal buttonhole.

Follow the steps shown in Photos 11–13 by first making a slip knot and placing it on the right-hand needle. Knit into that first stitch. Leaving it on the needle, pull the loop through and twist it around (away from you), then place it on the left-hand needle.

Step 1: Insert the right-hand needle between the first and second stitch, bring the yarn around the needle as if to knit and pull the resulting loop out, as demonstrated in Photo 11.

Step 2: Twist the loop away from you as shown in Photo 12.

Step 3: Place it on the left-hand needle as shown in Photo 13.

Repeat Steps 1–3, always working between the last two stitches on the left-hand needle. After finishing the cable cast-on, you will be ready to work a right side row.

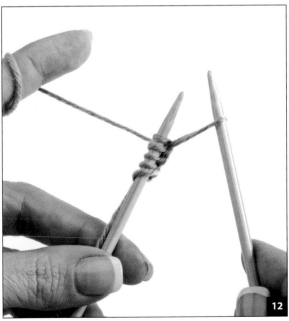

CAST-ON TIP

How long a tail do you need for a Long-Tail Cast-On? Unless you're working with a very thick yarn, an inch per stitch will provide more than enough. Also make sure that the tail end is over your thumb, and the ball end is over your finger—you use them up at different rates. The yarn that's going onto the needle is the yarn from your forefinger, and it's making the first row of stitches. The next row will be a wrong side row, so if you are working stockinette stitch, purl that row.

Knitted Cast-On

This is a variation of the cable cast-on. The only difference is that you continue to knit into the stitches, rather than between the stitches. Although simple, it's not suitable for most uses; it creates a very loose edge that is marked by large loops at the bottom. It is sometimes used for lace stitch patterns where a firm edge is not desirable.

Provisional Cast-Ons

These cast-ons have a very specific purpose: They are used when you'll need to pick up live stitch loops and start working them in the other direction. For example, they are often used when a decorative edging is going to be added to the bottom of a piece.

There are a number of ways to work a provisional cast-on—here are 3 of them:

Scrap yarn method

Cut a length of thick scrap yarn in a contrasting color. You may want to use a needle a couple sizes larger than your project needle.

By following the steps and Photos 14–18, make a slip knot with the working yarn and place it on the

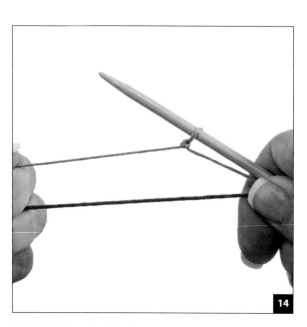

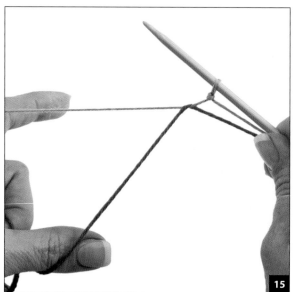

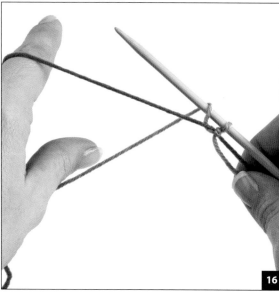

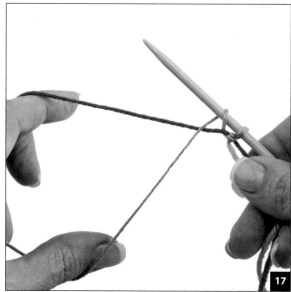

needle. Hold the scrap yarn and the working yarn together as shown in Photo 14.

Step 1: Wrap the working yarn around the front and under the scrap yarn as Photo 15 demonstrates.

Step 2 Carry the working yarn over the front of the needle and around the back as shown in Photo 16.

Repeat Steps 1 and 2 as shown in Photos 17 and 18.

You'll notice that you get loops both on the needle and on the scrap yarn. When you're ready to work the "lower" stitches, carefully remove the scrap yarn stitch by stitch and put the exposed stitches on a new needle.

Crochet hook method

You'll need a crochet hook that's similar in size to your working knitting needles and a length of smooth scrap yarn (mercerized cotton is good).

To start: Follow the steps and Photos 19–22. With the scrap yarn, make a slip knot near the end of the yarn, and place it on your crochet hook. Hold the scrap yarn under the knitting needle as shown in Photo 19.

Step 1: With the crochet hook, grab the scrap yarn and pull a loop over the knitting needle as shown in Photo 20, and through the loop on your crochet hook as in Photo 21.

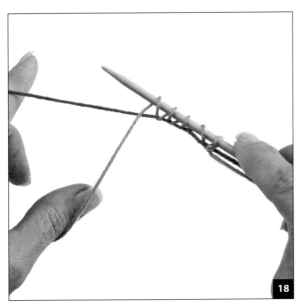

Step 2: Bring the yarn back under the knitting needle as in Photo 22.

Repeat Steps 1 and 2 until you've cast on one stitch fewer than you need. Put the loop from the crochet hook onto your knitting needle as the final stitch. Cut the waste yarn and mark the tail with a knot. Using your project yarn, work into those loops as normal. As above, when you're ready to work the "lower" stitches, carefully remove the scrap yarn stitch by stitch, pulling from the knotted end of the scrap yarn and put the exposed stitches on a new needle.

Crochet hook and scrap-yarn method

There is another way to work a provisional cast-on using a crochet hook and scrap yarn that is functionally the same as the method above. Using a crochet hook at least as large (or larger) than your working knitting needles, make a crochet chain that is several stitches longer than your desired number of cast-on stitches. Put a knot in the end tail of the chain. Now, with your project yarn, pick up and knit the required number of stitches in the bumps forming the "spine" of the chain. When you are ready to work in the other direction, "un-zip" the chain, beginning at the knotted end, and place the live stitches on your knitting needle.

Note: *You will notice that when you put the live stitches from the provisional cast-on onto your knitting needle, you will be short 1 stitch. This is because you are working in the downward loops that are formed between the stitches that were worked up—there is 1 fewer downward loop than upward loop. Not to worry. If it is important to have the original stitch count, just make a new stitch on your first row by working into an edge loop or by working an invisible increase anywhere on that row.*

Standard Bind-Off

This is straightforward and suitable for most uses, as shown in Photos 23–24.

To start: Knit the first stitch.

Step 1: Knit the next stitch.

Step 2: Lift the first stitch on the right-hand needle over the second stitch on the needle as shown in Photo 23, and all the way off as shown in Photo 24.

Repeat Steps 1 and 2 until one stitch remains. Cut the yarn, leaving a good length of tail, and pull it through the final stitch to finish.

The challenge with this bind-off is that it's often worked too tightly. Always use a larger needle (preferably a couple sizes larger) in your right hand to work the bind-off.

3-Needle Bind-Off

With right sides together and needles parallel, using a 3rd needle, knit together a stitch from the front needle with 1 from the back. *Knit together a stitch from the front and back needles, and slip the first stitch over the 2nd to bind off. Repeat from * across, then fasten off last stitch.

Sewn Bind-Off

This bind-off is terrific for garter stitch and mirrors a long-tail cast-on edge. It's a much stretchier edge than a standard bind-off. There are two minor drawbacks: It requires you to cut enough yarn (about 3–4 times the width of the fabric), and you have to have a yarn needle handy. Photos 25–27 demonstrate the four steps for this style of bind-off.

To start: Cut the yarn, leaving a tail about three times the width of the row you're binding off. Thread a blunt-end tapestry needle.

Step 1: Feed the needle through the first two stitches, as if to purl as in Photo 25.

Step 2: Pull the yarn through.

Step 3: Feed the needle through the first stitch as if to knit as Photo 26 illustrates.

Step 4: Pull the yarn through and slip the stitch off the needle as shown in Photo 27.

Repeat Steps 1–4 until one stitch remains. Cut the yarn, leaving a good length of tail, and pull it through the final stitch to finish.

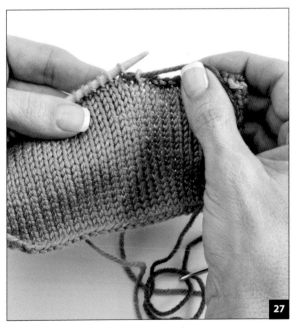

Decrease Bind-Off

The kind of bind-off shown in Photos 28 and 29 is stretchier than the standard bind-off, but is still very easy to work, and has a nice, low-profile edge. This bind-off is not suitable for bound-off edges along which the knitter will be picking up stitches, but it can be flexible and decorative.

Knit version:

Step 1: Knit 2 stitches together as shown in Photo 28.

Step 2: Slip the resulting stitch back to the left-hand needle, making sure it's not twisted.

Repeat Steps 1 and 2 until one stitch remains. Cut the yarn, leaving a good length of tail, and pull it through the final stitch to finish.

Purl version:

Purl the stitches together rather than knitting them.

COUNTING TIP

Count the "lifting over," not the stitches you've worked. To bind off one stitch, you have to knit 2. For example, if a pattern says to "k12, bind off 4, k12," work as follows: Knit 12 sts, then knit 2 more stitches before you start lifting over; after you have lifted 4 stitches over (4 bound-off stitches), you will have 1 stitch following the bind-off on your right-hand needle—this is counted as the first stitch of the last "k12," so knit 11 more stitches for the "k12."

Russian Lace Bind-Off

Photos 30–33 demonstrate the stretchiest of the bind-offs. It is useful when you need a lot of stretch in your piece, such as for lace or the cuff of toe-up socks. It is a fairly prominent bind-off. The purl version is the stretchier of the two, but also the most visible.

Knit version:

To start: Knit 2 as shown in Photo 30.

Step 1: Slip both stitches back from the right-hand needle to the left-hand needle, making sure you don't twist them as shown in Photo 31.

Step 2: Knit those two stitches together as shown in Photo 32.

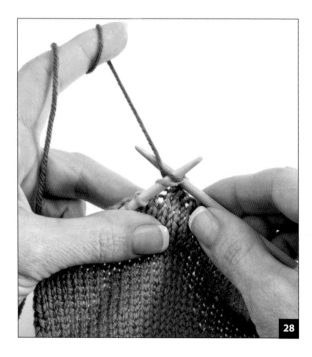

28

29

Step 3: Knit a stitch, so that there are two on the right-hand needle as shown in Photo 33.

Repeat Steps 1–3 until one stitch remains. Cut the yarn, leaving a good length of tail, and pull it through the final stitch to finish.

Purl version:

Purl the stitches rather than knitting them. ∎

BIND-OFF TIP

Instructions will often say to "bind off in pattern." This means that you work the stitches in the pattern stitch as you're binding off, e.g., in ribbing, knit the knit stitches and purl the purl stitches. It looks much better and is more elastic.

SPECIAL CAST-ON & BIND-OFF METHODS

Blocking Fundamentals

By Jennifer Hagan

Good blocking technique for the hand knitter is essential for a perfectly finished project.

Why should every knitter block his or her hand knits, at least most of the time? Simple—blocking gives that hard-earned project its final touch, a professional-looking finish. We all know that hand knitting an adult sweater can take months, and sometimes even years to complete. Bring that project home with one final step, the one that gives you the most pride in your hard work. It's really not that difficult, and with the right tools and methods, you can make your hand-knit projects much more satisfying.

Equipment

First of all, let's look at some of the basic equipment you'll need to block a garment. You can start with a package of rust-proof straight pins, some towels, and a spare bed or ironing board for small items. The most important factors are having a flat space free from traffic and an area with good ventilation.

Blocking Board

Even when you do have that spare bed or expansive carpeted area in your home, if you're serious about blocking, it's a good idea to either purchase or make your own blocking board. There are many styles available for purchase, including modular ones that can be broken down piece by piece and reassembled to suit the particular piece being blocked.

Visit your local sewing supply or craft store, and you'll find a cutting board or blocking board to fit your needs. Just make sure the blocking board material is waterproof and nontoxic, and that it will take the wear and tear of sticking pins into it—lots of pins.

If you'd like to make your own blocking board, it can be a fun project. First, buy a piece of plywood about ¼ inch thick from your local building supply store, where it may be cut to your specifications. A 3 x 5 foot board works quite well for blocking sweaters. Next, visit your sewing supply or craft store for some batting and fabric. You will need a piece of batting 1 inch or more thick and large enough to fit your board. Choose a 2-yard piece of 100 percent cotton fabric, making sure the fabric is at least 48 inches wide. If your fabric store carries gingham or other fabric that already has a grid, even better! You will also need a staple gun and some staples. An optional step in the process is gluing the batting to the board, so a hot-glue gun and some glue sticks will come in handy. Now you're ready to make your own board.

Lay the batting out on the board to fit, trimming around the edges if needed. Working a small area at a time, apply hot glue to the board with your glue gun and gently smooth the batting down on top of it. This will keep the batting from shifting around on the board with use. Take your cotton fabric and smooth it out on a flat surface, right side down. The floor works well for this step, but if you have a table top large enough, that works too. Flip the board (with batting attached) onto the fabric, batting-side down against the fabric, making sure to position the board in the middle with even margins of fabric on all sides. Trim fabric as needed. Starting at one long side of the board, begin turning up the fabric edges and applying staples about 2 inches apart. Work only one area at a time. Move to the opposite side of the board and apply the same number of staples in the same manner. Repeat this process until you have stapled all sides, up to about 3 inches away from each of the four corners. Now, fold the fabric in at each corner to make a neat edge and staple securely. Flip blocking board over, and you're ready to block.

Yardstick

Another piece of equipment needed for blocking is a yardstick and perhaps a ruler. It is best not to use a tape measure to determine your garment's dimensions when blocking because a tape measure can stretch. A yardstick or ruler provides a more stable reference. Lay the item out and pin it to match the finished measurements for the piece.

Pins

It matters a great deal which kind of pins you use to block damp knitted items. You want to choose pins that won't rust and have heads large enough not to become lost in your stitches. Stainless steel pins work well, and many knitters swear by the quilting pins with glass or plastic heads. T-pins made from stainless steel work well too, and they come in different sizes. Longer T-pins with larger heads will be perfect for thicker projects knit with bulky yarn and for felted (or fulled) items. To block more delicate projects like lace shawls, a smaller pin works best.

Blocking Wires

For lace blocking, a set of blocking wires will be one of your best investments. Many avid lace knitters use blocking wires to give their large shawls and scarves the perfect finish. Blocking wires are not just for lace, though. They can also help with straight edges on sweaters.

A couple of other items that may come in handy are a spray bottle and some cotton cloth.

Methods

Most of the methods discussed in this section involve wetting your knitted fabric. It is a good idea to try this on your gauge swatch first. Some fibers change dramatically when water is applied, especially if completely immersed in water as opposed to simply misting. Blocking your gauge swatch can give you advanced warning of this.

Wet Blocking

For the serious blocker, nothing works better than wet blocking. Wet blocking is the process of

completely immersing the knitted project in a bath before laying it out to block. Here's the method.

Wash your hand knits one at a time, unless you are working with several pieces knit with the same yarn in the same color. Fill an appropriately-sized sink with cold or lukewarm water and a teaspoon of delicate laundry detergent, wool wash or baby shampoo. Place your knitted item into the water and gently squeeze to release the dirt. Do not rub or agitate the fabric. Allow the sweater to soak for about an hour so that the water can completely penetrate each part of the fabric. When you are ready to rinse, drain the water from the sink, gently press out most of the water in the sweater, and fill the sink again with clean, cold or lukewarm water. Swish the sweater around in the water to release the soap and dirt. Repeat the rinse as many times as needed until the water remains clear. Drain the sink and press out as much water as you can without agitating the sweater. You should never wring out excess water nor should you lift the knitting out

of the sink by one end—you will stretch the fabric. Gently lift the entire object out of the sink as a whole with both hands.

Have several large towels on hand (beach towels or large bath towels work very well), and lay the sweater down on a towel. Roll the towel up and gently press out the moisture from the sweater. Repeat with fresh, dry towels until the sweater feels only slightly damp. Using your yardstick or ruler, block the item out to the finished measurements in the pattern. Measure as you go, pinning vital points as shown in Photo 1, by width first and then by height, and then alternating between the two until you have placed pins at least 1 inch evenly apart along all edges of your object, all the while smoothing the entire surface with a flat palm. Make sure to place enough pins along the edges so that you do not cause scalloping.

Your objective is to produce a straight or curved edge where appropriate as illustrated in both Photo 1 and Photo 2. If the item is edged in a type of ribbing that is meant to pull in, do not pin out this ribbing. Smooth out the rib stitches as best you can without widening them.

Allow your blocked item to dry completely away from direct sunlight and direct heat before removing the pins and taking it up from the blocking surface. This may take from a few hours to a couple of days, depending on fiber type. Directing a small fan at the fabric being

completely blocked and assembled. This is one instance for pressing the item.

Lay your knitted item wrong side out on a surface that's safe for pressing. Cover the knitting with a piece of cotton cloth. A pillowcase works well for this. Heat your iron to the correct setting for the fabric and gently press, always making sure that the iron never comes in direct contact with the knitted fabric. Do not move the iron back

until the entire piece has been pressed. Do not press ribbing or any beading, elastic, buttons, zippers or trim that you may have added to your knitted piece.

Steaming

You can also steam the fabric with your household iron. Consult the yarn label first to confirm that the fiber may be steamed. Some manufacturers will recommend only pressing with a dry cloth. Lay the item out on a safe surface for working—the ironing board is designed for this. You can also use your blocking board or any flat surface covered by a few layers of toweling. You can either pin the garment to its dimensions before you steam or pin as you go along. Some garments will only lend themselves to being shaped successfully after they become at least a little damp.

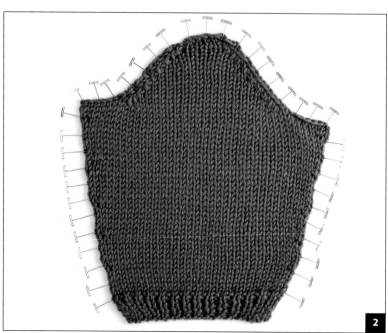

Fill your iron with clean water and turn it to the steam setting. Dampen a piece of cotton fabric, and lay it on top of the knitted fabric. When the iron is hot, hold it above the surface of the knitted item and move it over every area without touching the iron to the cotton fabric. You just want the steam to flow through the cotton into the knitting. Repeat until the cotton fabric is dry. When you have achieved your desired result, leave the item to cool and

blocked can greatly speed up the drying process.

If you do not have time to give your knitted item a complete bath, the same process may also be followed by using a spray bottle to simply spritz the fabric. Follow all other steps in the same manner.

Pressing

Sometimes your knitted item may only need a light block after wearing just to freshen it. Other times, only the seams of a garment may need blocking after all the pieces have been

and forth or apply pressure, as when ironing woven fabrics. Apply the iron gently to the surface, lift, move to another area, and repeat

> ### GAUGE TIP
>
> **Gauge should be checked before beginning any knitting project.** The best way to do this is to make a gauge swatch which represents all the stitch patterns in your project, or at least stockinette stitch. Refer to Making the Gauge Swatch, page 12 for more details. A gauge swatch should never be measured until it has been blocked, especially when worked in one of the stitch patterns, refer to Stitch Pattern, under the Fiber Type section of this chapter. Refer to your particular pattern, however, for specific instructions for achieving gauge.

dry before removing it from your blocking surface.

A steamer is another good investment for blocking. Steaming finished knits can lend a professional look without all the bother of wet blocking or even pressing. Follow the directions on the steamer as well as the care instructions for the yarn.

Variables

Since knitting can produce so many different types of items that need blocking, there are some variables to discuss.

Garment Structure

Sweaters knit in the round need to be blocked differently than those knit in flat pieces. It is easier to block each piece of a flat knit before assembling it because you are dealing with one layer of fabric. A sweater knit in the round is two layers thick and will take longer to dry. Also, when pinning out this type of sweater, extra care must be taken to make sure the edges are laid out correctly and that the back side of the fabric is not bunched and crooked. Smooth out the wrinkles on the back side of the garment before laying it on your surface, front side up. While the garment is damp, certain size adjustments may be made. Damp wool, for example, can be stretched to make up for unexpected differences in length and width. It may also be eased to be a bit smaller while blocking. You don't have to be satisfied with a garment's condition as soon as it comes off the needles. These adjustments can make your garment just as you dreamed it would be.

Sweaters that are knit in separate pieces, and then assembled, benefit from being blocked twice. Block each piece before assembling in order to produce smooth, even edges for seaming. Blocking will also ensure that the edges to be seamed on coordinating pieces of the garment are the same lengths and widths, such as the two front pieces of a cardigan. As in the Photo 3 example, after assembly, you may need to wet block the sweater again, especially if complicated edges have been added after assembly. The collar and possibly button and buttonhole bands may need an extra finish. If not, then the seams may be pressed or steamed.

Fiber Type

Just as yarns of various fibers knit up differently, they respond to blocking differently as well. Be very familiar with the fiber content of the yarn used in your project. It's easiest to determine

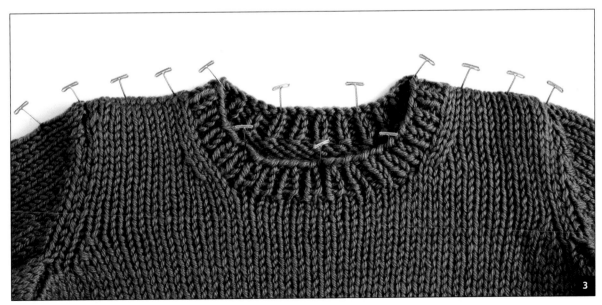

3

the best care techniques for yarns made from a single fiber. Many yarns contain a blend of fibers, however, and must be given more consideration. Refer to the yarn's label for care instructions. Here are some general guidelines to follow, remembering that those fibers which may be wet blocked will respond to all the other methods as well.

Animal or protein fibers are the easiest to block and all may be wet blocked. Wool responds beautifully to wet blocking, because it helps the fabric to relax into its true form. Be careful with alpaca, llama and silk, however, because they have a tendency to stretch even when dry and may not retain their shape if stretched too much while wet. Mohair and angora are especially fuzzy fibers which may need a gentle brushing to release some of the fibers after they have been blocked.

Plant or cellulose fibers will produce varying results when blocked. Linen and hemp favor water, and may actually benefit from wet blocking. Cotton has no memory and will stretch out of shape if you do not handle it carefully. Cotton also takes much longer to dry than animal fibers. Cellulose fibers usually have little or no elasticity, and this needs to be considered when choosing them for any knitting project. Blocking will solve few problems

4

in a fiber with these qualities. A garment made with any of these fibers may also be machine washed and dried, as long as you remember to take it out of the dryer before it's completely dry and to finish the garment by laying it out to dry. Never hang any knitted item to dry, especially one made with cellulose fiber.

Cellulose fibers (i.e. rayons), which classify somewhere between the plant fibers and the man-made

fibers, respond in a limited way to wetting and blocking. These materials have been reconstituted into fiber from soy, corn, milk, wood, seaweed, bamboo, etc., and may shrink and weaken with washing.

Synthetic or man-made fibers are usually machine washable and may benefit from pinning and spritzing. Refer to the care instructions on the yarn label with these fibers especially. This goes double for novelty yarns, which almost always include man-made fiber. These are the only types of fibers that may benefit from dry cleaning as long as the care instructions recommend it.

Cellulosic and synthetic fibers should never be ironed because they can melt. Acrylic becomes lifeless after being steamed, which is why steaming acrylic

POSITIONING TIP

Usually, you will need to block your garment, no matter the method, right side up. The stitch patterns have most likely been worked to make this the more attractive side, so you do not want to flatten or distort those stitch patterns by laying them face down on your blocking surface. This step may vary according to the chosen blocking process. For example, sometimes pressing and steaming should be done with the fabric wrong side out.

5

4 and 5. In the swatches pictured, each shows an unblocked swatch on top, and a blocked below. Clearly, there is a dramatic difference between the blocked swatches and the unblocked swatches. After blocking, both of these examples relax dramatically in width and a little in height when wet blocked. Just imagine what a difference this would make in the fit and presentation of a cabled or lace garment.

Fair Isle and other color-work stitch patterns may have an uneven look when finished because the stitches may have been stretched here and there due to the carrying of the yarn across the back of the fabric. Blocking will help to even out these stitch patterns.

A stitch pattern which is worked with the intention of creating a raised or embellished surface must be blocked carefully. You don't want to spend the time working a complicated pattern for a certain effect only to lose it in the blocking process. Once your item is pinned out, you can manipulate the stitches to achieve the effect needed. ■

is called "killing it." All of the fibers mentioned will produce a myriad of results when blended. With a fiber blend, it is especially important to refer to the care instructions given by the manufacturer.

Stitch Pattern

With so many stitch patterns to chose from, knitters are always challenged to learn new techniques. The same is true of learning how to present each type of stitch pattern in its best light by blocking it correctly. Some types of stitch patterns certainly call for more rigorous blocking than others.

Since cable and lace stitch patterns tend to shrink and distort the knitted fabric, it is critical to block them carefully. You can see how this is the case in Photo examples

CONTINUED CARE

Once you have blocked a knitted item thoroughly, you may not need to repeat the entire process for future washings. You may find that if you have given your hand-knit sweater a full bath and a thorough blocking, all that is needed after consecutive washings is to smooth your freshly-washed sweater out onto the blocking board and to allow it to dry completely. A sweater screen works well for this. You do need to wash your hand knits regularly, because little winged creatures will nest in the dirt and food particles in them. Take good care of your hand knitted art and it will last as long as you do.

Construction Essentials: Garment Assembly, Seaming & Weaving Methods

By Kate Atherley

Proper seaming isn't hard—in fact, it's surprisingly easy; you just have to know which technique to use in which situation.

Many knitters, especially the less experienced, are attracted to one-piece garments because of the limited finishing required. Although these designs can be fun to knit, the construction limits the style and fit choices. In addition, the lack of seams makes them prone to stretching and sagging, particularly if worked in a heavy yarn. A pieced garment provides advantages: There are more options for style and fit, and the seams themselves help the garment retain its structure. Seamed garments are often easier to adapt and modify too. The benefits of a pieced garment definitely outweigh the finishing effort.

The correct seaming technique can make all the difference in the look of the finished garment. No matter how beautifully it's been knitted, a poorly seamed garment just won't look good. Proper seaming isn't hard—in fact, it's surprisingly easy; you just have to know which technique to use in which situation.

Order of Assembly

Usually, the shoulders of a garment are put together first. The collar—and for a cardigan, the front edgings—is next. Then, the sleeves are attached, and finally the side and sleeve seams are sewn.

For a raglan-sleeve design, the sleeves are sewn to the body first because they form the shoulders. Then, the collar/neckline edging is worked, and finally the side and sleeve seams are sewn.

General Tips

Make sure you've blocked the pieces before you start seaming. They will lie flatter and be easier to work with. In addition, you want to make sure that any shrinking or stretching has taken place before you seam—if the garment shrinks after you seam it up, the seams can pull or pucker.

Before you start sewing, safety pin the pieces together to line everything up. This will help you with the seaming, and it will also give you an opportunity to try on the garment. Seeing a

sweater assembled provides good encouragement to finish it up!

When sewing the sleeve and side seams, work from the lower edges up to the underarm, because any unevenness can be hidden under the arm.

The best yarn for seaming is smooth, washable and colorfast. Although you can sew most seams with the project yarn, in some cases this is not the appropriate choice. Fuzzy or textured yarns are difficult to sew with; a yarn that is not very tightly spun will fray and break as you pull it through the stitches while seaming. If you are working with a bulky yarn, your seams may get too thick. Sock yarn is a great choice because it's thin, strong and smooth. While it's desirable to match the color of the main fabric, it's not critical that it be exactly the same color because for most types of seams, the sewing yarn isn't visible.

Should you use your ends or new lengths of yarn for seaming? If you're going to use a different type of yarn entirely, then obviously you need to cut new lengths of yarn for seaming. If you decide to undo the garment in the future, then it's better to sew with new lengths of yarn. Otherwise, feel free to use the ends from where you started and ended balls. You'd have to weave them in anyway!

If you're starting with a new length of yarn, you don't need to make knots, just leave about a 4-inch tail, and then weave that in when you're done.

And perhaps the most important tip of all: Throw out everything you know about sewing fabric. The techniques for seaming hand-knits are entirely different.

Mattress Stitch Seam

This is an invisible method for vertical seams. It's used anywhere you need to seam together the side edges of two pieces—most often when joining the fronts and backs of garments.

It's very easy, and when done right, it makes the join look seamless. It's nice and firm, but doesn't pucker the fabric, and it's not bulky. It's the only technique you should use for vertical seams.

On Stockinette Stitch

Line up the pieces side by side, with right sides facing. Loosely pin them together with safety pins at about 4-inch intervals to ensure that you keep them even. Cut a 12-inch length of yarn, and thread your darning needle. Look carefully at the edge of your piece. The first stitch is always awkward—just ignore that. You want to be working between the first and second stitches of the pieces.

With your yarn needle, pick up the bar between the first and second

stitches of the first row on the right piece.

Pick up the corresponding bar on the left piece as shown in Photo 1.

Alternate sides, picking up every bar, one for one. Pull the seam tight as you go, so that the pieces line up together. For a perfectly vertical seam, make sure that you

stay in the same column, between the first and second stitches.

On Garter Stitch and Reverse Stockinette Stitch

Instead of picking up bars between the stitches, pick up the downwards loops of the purl stitches on one side, the upwards loops on the other side as the Photo 2 example shows.

When you seam with mattress stitch, the edge stitch of both pieces disappears into the seam. If you are working ribbing, you will want to take that into account. Make sure that there is a single knit stitch on the edge of each piece, and that the ribbing flows between the second to last stitch on the right piece and the second stitch on the left piece. For example, if you're working K2, P2 Rib, the piece on the right should end with k2, and the piece on the left should start with k2, so that when you join them together, you see one knit stitch from each side, forming a perfect K2, P2 Rib. If you're working K1, P1 Rib, the first piece should end with p1, k1, and the second should start with k2, so that when the two knit stitches on the edges disappear, the ribbing flows from a p1 on the right piece to a k1 on the left piece.

Invisible Horizontal Seam

This is the technique for invisible horizontal seams—for joining cast-on and bound-off edges—and is typically used for joining shoulders. It can be used in two ways: Left loose, it creates a seamless join; pulled tight, it creates a visible, but neat and firm join. For shoulder seams, I recommend pulling it tight to ensure it doesn't stretch or sag. You must have the same number of stitches on both edges.

Referring to Photo 3, line up the pieces with the right sides facing, with the edges to be seamed touching. Examine the lower piece—you'll see stitches oriented so that the "v"s are upside down, the narrow point is at the top edge. On the upper piece, notice the stitches oriented so that the narrow points of the "v"s are at the bottom.

Step 1. Run your darning needle under the point at the top of the lower piece.

Step 2. Then, run your darning needle under the point of the corresponding "v" at the bottom of the upper piece.

Continue, alternating sides. Don't skip a stitch.

The process is the same for garter stitch or reverse stocking stitch, you just have to look a bit more closely to find the points of the "v"s.

Invisible Vertical to Horizontal

Another invisible seaming method, this is a combination of the above two methods. It's used most often for sewing sleeves—particularly drop sleeves that are straight across the top—onto the garment body. It's also used for sewing on button bands or anywhere that you need to attach two pieces at a right angle.

You'll work one piece vertically, picking up the bars, and one piece horizontally, working under the point (bottoms) of the "v"s. Pin out the pieces before you begin.

3

Since there are more rows to the inch than stitches (remember your gauge), you'll need to accommodate that difference so that the edge doesn't cause one side to pucker. When working stockinette stitch (or reverse stockinette stitch), for every third "v" point you pick up, pick up 2 bars rather than one as Photo 4 illustrates. For other stitch patterns, such as garter stitch, pinning the two pieces together will give you a good sense of how you'll need to ease the two pieces together.

Seaming Curved Edges

When you're sewing a set-in sleeve or shaped sleeve cap into the armhole, as in the example in Photo 5, you're typically working along a curved edge that's neither perfectly vertical nor perfectly horizontal. You'll need to adjust your technique as you go to match the alignment of the stitches. A typical set-in sleeve seam will use some combination of all three techniques outlined above.

When you're seaming the lower portion of the seam, at the initial bind-offs for the armhole shaping, you'll use a horizontal seam. At the uppermost portion, the top of the shoulder, you'll use the horizontal to vertical seam. In between, on the slope, you'll be working mattress stitch, accommodating the decreases.

Grafting, a.k.a. Kitchener Stitch

Grafting is used for joining together live stitches—that is, stitches that have not been bound off. It's a horizontal join like the one previously discussed. When worked with the same yarn as the main fabric and with careful tension, it's invisible from both the right and wrong sides. You must have the same number of stitches on both edges.

Photo 6 illustrates the results of the Grafting/Kitchener stitch on Stockinette stitch, and how it makes a soft and flexible edge. It's often used to close up the toes of socks or the tops of mittens, or to join together pieces of lace scarves and shawls. It should not be used for joining shoulders on a sleeved garment because it will not give enough support for the weight of the sleeves, and the shoulders will stretch out.

To start, line up the two pieces on the needles with right sides facing you.

Cut the working yarn so it's about three times the width of the row, and thread your darning needle. Insert the darning needle purlwise through the first stitch on the front needle, and pull the yarn through. Then, insert the darning needle knitwise through the first stitch on the back needle, and pull the yarn through.

Step 1. Insert the darning needle knitwise through the first stitch on the front needle. Pull the yarn through and slip the stitch off the needle as demonstrated in Photo 7.

Step 2. Referring to Photo 8, insert the darning needle purlwise through the (new) first stitch on the front needle, and pull the yarn through.

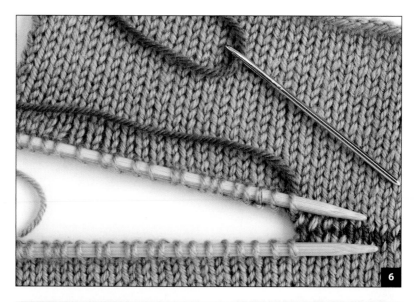

Step 3. As shown in Photo 9, insert the darning needle purlwise through the first stitch on the back needle. Pull the yarn through and slip the stitch off the needle.

Step 4. Insert the darning needle knitwise through the (new) first stitch on the back needle, and pull the yarn through as in Photo 10.

Repeat Steps 1–4.

You'll see that you're following the path of a new row of stitches with your darning needle.

As you're working, make sure to carefully pull the yarn so that the tension of these new stitches matches that of the knitted stitches.

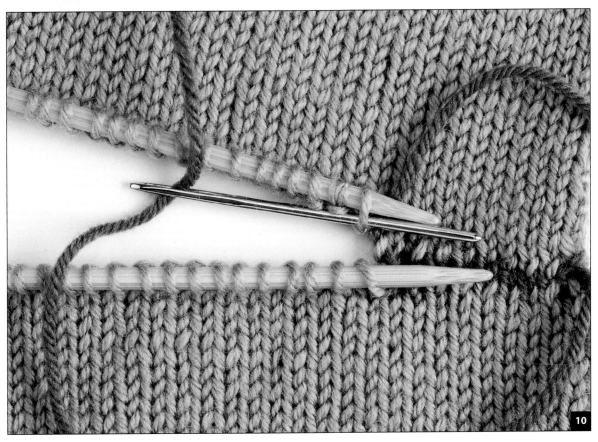

Seaming With Stripes and Color

When seaming with stripes and color, make sure that the yarn with which you are sewing doesn't show through the other colors; for example, don't sew with black yarn if it reads through white stripes.

Use the same techniques, and do take time to pin the pieces together carefully before you start to make sure you're lining up the stripes.

Crochet Seams

Crochet seams are quick and easy, but they can be very bulky. They're best used for pillows and afghans rather than garments. Slip stitch is the least bulky and works well to join together two pieces in a fold, for example the fronts and backs of a pillow or the sides of a bag. Single crochet works well for joining flat pieces, like pieces of an afghan.

Weaving in Ends

Weaving in ends often strikes fear in the heart of knitters. No need—not only is it very simple, but in many cases it's actually optional! You need to weave in your ends mostly for cosmetic reasons. As long as you've joined the yarn securely and it's not visible from the right side, then you don't need to worry about it.

Of course, if the item you're making is for a gift, then you will likely want to take more care to tidy it up.

Which End?

You will have loose ends at a number of places in your knitting: at one edge of each cast-on and bind-off row and at spots where

VERTICAL SEAMING TIP

Vertical seaming on pieces with shaping. If there are increases or decreases right at the beginning and end of the rows, you'll need to take those into account as you work. When you encounter an increase or a decrease, just step out one full stitch to the next column.

you've joined a new ball of yarn. Longer tails can be used for seaming, as required; refer to page 17 for more information.

The Yarn Makes a Difference

The degree of effort you need to make is also determined by the type of yarn you're using. If you're using a wool fiber that will felt, you can be a bit more relaxed about it. Wearing the piece will cause the ends to felt nicely into the fabric and all will be secure.

If you are going to weave in the ends of a superwash wool, cotton or other non-felting yarn, make sure you weave in at least 4 inches so they don't work their way out.

Knots–Why Not?

It's accepted wisdom that you shouldn't make knots, but the reason why isn't often understood. The problem with knots is that they can come undone, particularly if the ends are cut very short. They also have a terrible habit of popping out to the front of your work.

If you encounter a knot in the yarn you're working with, undo it and proceed as though you're joining a new ball.

And don't knot your ends when you join—just leave yourself a decent tail. Whether you weave the ends in or not, as long as

you've joined the new yarn securely, it will hold nicely.

The Best Solution

The best solution is to weave ends into seams when you can. If you're working a garment in pieces, join any new yarn at the beginning of a new row, and the tails will be hanging right at the edges, ready to be woven into the seams (or used for seaming).

The ends from the cast-on and bind-off will also conveniently be at the edges of the piece. When working neckline shaping, you often have to bind off in the middle of a row, but usually some kind of collar or neckline treatment will be added later and that edge also creates a nice spot for weaving in ends.

Of course, if you're working something in the round, you'll have no choice but to join yarn in the middle. Just try to do it somewhere inconspicuous—on the back, or below where the sleeves will be.

General Guidelines

A blunt-tipped darning needle is required. You don't want to split the yarn; you want to weave neatly around the stitches.

If it's not possible to weave ends into a seam, try to weave them in somewhere reasonably hidden—

at the back or under the arms. Ribbing is a great place to hide your ends too. The purl ribs pull to the inside of the work, and so even if your ends aren't tidy, at least they're not prominent.

Weaving on Stockinette and Garter Stitch

Thread your darning needle with your yarn tail, and run the tail through the back loops of the stitches. As shown in Photos 11 and 12, work diagonally along the piece. If you work vertically it can show through, and if you work horizontally, it can cause the row to pucker. Weave at least a couple of inches in one direction, and then another couple of inches in another. Gently pull the fabric a bit to even it all out, and cut off the end.

Note: Before you cut the yarn end off, turn the piece over to ensure that the tail can't be seen from the right side.

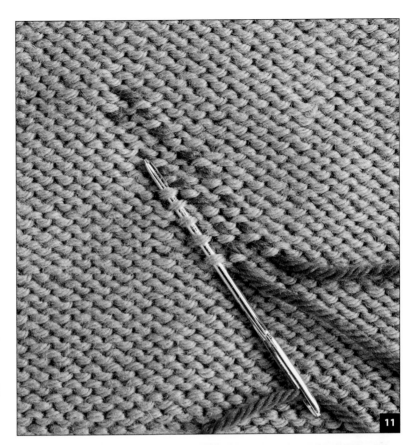

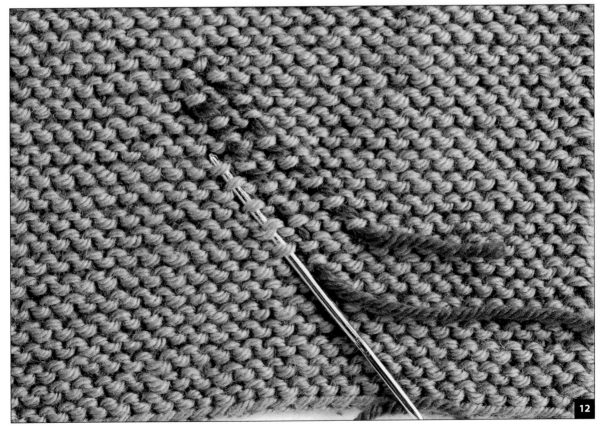

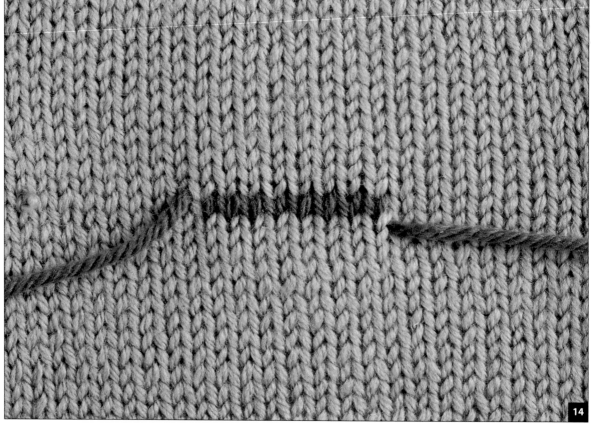

Weaving on Reverse Stockinette Stitch

When weaving on reverse stockinette stitch, as in the Photo 13 example, the process is the same, but there is a greater risk of the yarn showing through to the right side because of the way the stitches are made. Be careful to check that woven-in tails are not visible.

Weaving Into Ribbing and Cables

Weaving ends into ribbing and cables is easy—just weave the ends vertically into a knit rib on the wrong side (that is, a rib that shows as purls on the right side). Because these ribs pull to the back, even if you're not tidy, they won't be seen.

Special cases: Lace, slippery yarns and multiple colors

If you're working with a particularly slippery yarn like silk, or working a complex pattern stitch, like lace, your best bet for weaving in the ends is to use a duplicate stitch. With your tail threaded on your darning needle, working on the wrong side, follow the path of the stitches for at least a couple of inches, as shown in the Photo 14 example. Be careful to keep the tension even, matching the tension of the knitted stitches.

Note that if you do this, the tail being used for the duplicate stitch will be visible on the right side, so obviously, it's not suitable for weaving in lengths of contrasting colors.

If you're working with more than one color, weave the tail into a section of the same color. ∎

No-Nonsense Neckline & Collar Treatments

By Arenda Holladay

Care must be taken that the neckline is neatly worked both when knitting the garment and when finishing it.

The neckline is the most visible part of any garment because it frames the wearer's neck and face; therefore, a poorly finished neckline is very noticeable. Care must be taken that the neckline is neatly worked both when knitting the garment and when finishing it. If the neckline is not shaped with the final finished edge in mind, the end result may be disappointing.

While individual patterns specify how the neckline is shaped, an overview of the basic types of neckline shapings and some general rules for shaping them is helpful.

Neckline Shaping

There are four basic types of neckline shapings, as shown in Figures 1–4.

Boat

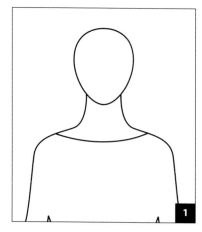

This neckline requires the least shaping. While some patterns call for center stitches to be bound off with a few decreases made at the neck edges, others just require all stitches to be bound off. Boat necks are a good choice for baby sweaters because babies' heads are proportionally larger than their bodies.

Square

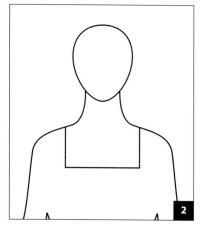

For square necklines, the center stitches are bound off and each side is worked separately with no decreases being made. This type of shaping is also used for the insertion of a front placket for vertical (polo) necklines, the only difference being that only a few stitches are bound off at the base of the neckline to accommodate the placket stitches.

Curved

The most common style of a curved neckline is the crew neck, which is usually about 2½ to 3 inches deep and is shaped over several rows. First, the center

NECKLINE SHAPING TIP

Plan for finishing while shaping the neckline by thinking about where you will pick up stitches. Be sure to leave the same number of selvage stitches at each neckline edge. To mirror the decreases on the neckline, use ssk decreases on one side and k2tog decrease on the other. The resulting garment will have a more professional appearance.

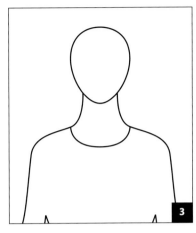

stitches are bound off or put on hold; many patterns require additional stitches to be bound off at both neck edges followed by a series of decreases. This method of shaping is also used for round or scoop necklines.

V-Neck

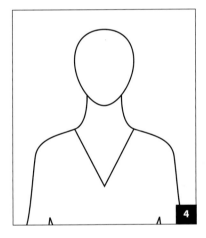

The center stitch or stitches are bound off and mirrored decreases are worked at the neck edges, generally every right-side row, every 4th row or every 6th row depending on the slant of the neckline.

General Rules

Patterns rarely provide specific information about neckline shaping. Often the instructions read something like this: "Bind off center 20 sts. Working both sides of the neck separately, dec 1 st at neck edge every right side row 4 times." Many instructions don't state how to work each side separately, where to place the decreases or what type of decreases to use. Many knitters find the instructions for how often to work the decreases confusing as well. These general rules apply to most types of necklines:

• Most knitters prefer to work both sides of the neckline at the same time. To do this, you must use another ball of yarn. Work the left-hand side (as worn) of the neckline first, then bind off the center stitches and work to the end of the row. When you turn the work, you are working the right-hand side (as worn) of the neckline. Since the center stitches have been bound off, attach another ball of yarn to work the left-hand side. It isn't necessary to tie a knot, but leave at least a 6-inch yarn tail.

• On the row following the neck bind-off, be sure to work one or two stitches as selvage stitches at each neck edge (do not use a slip-stitch selvage because you will not be able to pick up stitches neatly for a band). All decreases should be worked inside of these selvage stitches—after the selvage stitch(es) at the beginning of a row and before the selvage stitch(es) at the end of a row. Once again, this will ensure that you are able to pick up stitches for the neckband or to seam a band neatly. If the design has a stitch pattern, consider how to incorporate the decreases and the selvage stitches into the pattern. Try to make the stitch patterns match on either side of the neckline. For complicated stitch patterns, you may find that you need to bind off the stitches at the neck edge rather than work decreases.

• Rarely does a pattern specifically state which decreases to use. This is your decision. The most commonly used decreases are k2tog (which slants to the right) and ssk (which slants to the left). The neckline will look neater if mirrored decreases are used. This means that k2tog decreases are used on one side and ssk decreases are used on the other side. If you want the decreases to slant in the same direction as the neck, ssk decreases should be used on the right-hand side of the neckline (at the beginning of a row) and k2tog decreases should be used on the left-hand side (at the end of the row). When working color-work patterns (especially Fair Isle patterns), the color pattern will be maintained if the decreases are worked so that they lean toward the slope of the neck—k2tog at the beginning of a row and ssk at the end of a row. If working in a single color of yarn, mirrored decreases worked toward the slope of the neckline will be more noticeable, but can be very decorative.

• Pattern language describing how often to make the decreases can be confusing. When a pattern says to make decreases "every 4th row" or "every 6th row," it can seem that the decreases are to be made on the wrong side of the work. Work the decrease on the right side row. The first row after the decrease row is a WS row, the second row is a RS row, the third row is a WS row. The fourth row, a RS row, is the next decrease row.

Neckline Styles

There are many different styles of neckline finishing, but the basic types are bands, collars and hoods. These styles work well on either pullovers or cardigans and on many of the types of neckline shapings, as shown in Figures 5–8.

Bands

Bands are the most common type of neckline finishing and can be continuous, overlapping or extended.

Continuous Bands

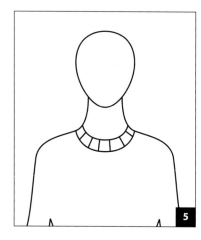

Continuous bands on pullovers are worked in the round on all stitches of the neckline. Continuous bands on cardigans are worked on all of the stitches of the neckline and the fronts at the same time.

Overlapping Bands

Overlapping bands are worked only on pullovers. Instead of working the bands in the round, they are worked back and forth after which the edges are sewn down along the bound-off stitches at the base of the neck.

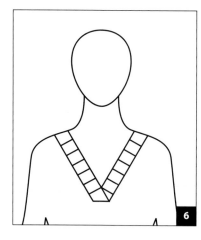

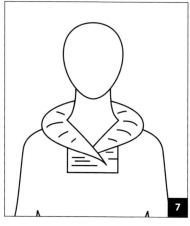

Extended Bands

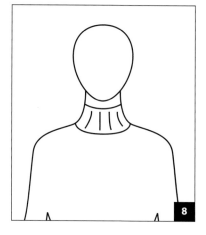

Turtlenecks, cowls and shawl collars fall into the extended-band category. These types of bands are wider than the other types and can be folded over. This means they must be wider at the outer edge. Different designers

handle this in a variety of ways. You may be instructed to increase the number of stitches, switch to a larger needle size or in the case of shawl collars, work a series of several short rows at the upper part of the neck.

Collars

Collars can be worked on either pullovers or cardigans. Some patterns specify that they be worked separately and then sewn in place using the appropriate seaming technique. Other patterns call for stitches to be picked up along the neckline. When this is the case, increases must be worked to shape the collar or it will not lay flat. The number of increases also determines how the collar's outer edge will angle. The first example in the illustration requires fewer increases. When a collar is worked for a polo-style neckline, the button and buttonhole band should be worked first.

Since collars are folded over, you should pick up stitches from the wrong side of the neckline.

For seamed collars, sew the pieces together so that the collar turns over with the right-side facing out; this is critical if the collar fabric isn't reversible

Hoods

Hoods can be worked either as an integral part of the garment or as a separate piece that is sewn on. When working an integrated hood, stitches are picked up along the neckline and worked to the desired length. Generally, increases are evenly spaced to accommodate the shape of the head and the top is either seamed or grafted. Another option is to shape the top of the hood with short rows, not unlike turning a sock heel. For a sewn-on hood, the bottom stitches are cast on, the hood fabric and shaping (if any) are worked, after which it's seamed up the back and sewn in place.

General Rules for Finishing Necklines

Whatever the style of the neckline finishing, if it is worked from stitches that are picked up along the neckline, some general rules apply. (If the neckline band or collar is worked separately and seamed, seaming techniques apply.) When, where and how many stitches to pick up are questions knitters frequently have when contemplating neckline finishing.

When? The neckline cannot be finished until the shoulders are seamed. Although some

pullover patterns specify that only one shoulder is seamed before stitches are picked up so that the neckband can be worked back and forth, it isn't necessary to do this. With the current popularity of circular needles and the "Magic Loop" technique, the neckline can be worked in the round, thus eliminating a band seam.

For a cardigan with front bands, the neckline band can be worked before or after the front bands are worked—it depends on the desired result.

Where? For continuous necklines on pullovers, begin at a shoulder seam. If you have to fudge the number of stitches you are picking up, this location will help hide the adjustment. For continuous bands on cardigans, begin on the right front with the right side facing.

Stitches are picked up along horizontal edges where stitches have been bound off, in vertical

edges (or rows) or along curved edges. When stitches are picked up in the wrong spot, the neckline can have a "homemade" rather than "handmade" appearance. This is a particular problem in places where there are "stair steps" from bound-off stitches, along curved edges or at the transition points of horizontal and vertical edges.

Horizontal edges: Do not pick up the stitches in the loops from the bound-off stitches. This places the stitches in the band between the stitches in the garment. Instead, pick up in the stitch immediately below the bind-off edge. This way, the band stitches are in the same column of stitches as in the garment. Follow this rule when picking up stitches in a "stair step." Don't pick up the stitch in the hole at the join of the stair step—this just leaves a bigger hole. As shown in Photo 1, pins are placed at the locations to pick up the stitches. Although it may look like there

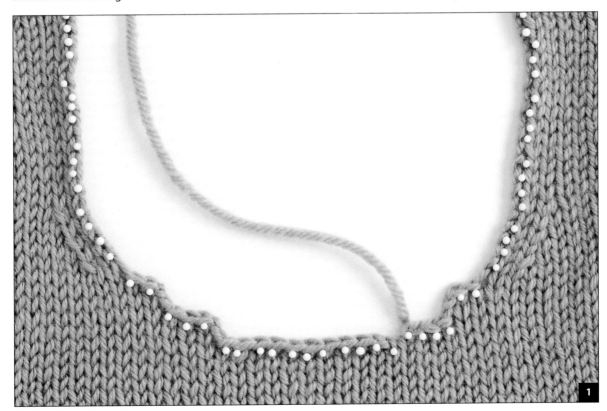

is too great a distance between the stitches in the curves of the neckline, the finished result proves this is not the case.

Vertical edges: Pick up stitches in the spaces between the horizontal bars which separate the selvage stitch and the column of stitches next to it. Mattress stitch seams are worked in this same place. The selvage stitch provides support for the band. Take care not to shift over half a stitch. There should be a column of full stitches next to the band. Pins mark these locations as shown on Photo 1 as well.

How Many? This question plagues many knitters. Most patterns specify the number of stitches to pick up, but what if this number doesn't work for the garment? What is important is that the band looks good, not that some particular number of stitches be picked up.

Horizontal edges: This is easy—pick up one stitch for every bound-off stitch.

Vertical edges: Picking up the correct number of stitches along a vertical edge is much trickier because stitches are generally wider than they are long. Consider a typical gauge statement: "24 sts and 32 rows = 4 inches," which means that 6 sts and 8 rows equal 1 inch. If you pick up one stitch for every row (every horizontal bar represents a row), the band will flare because there will be two more stitches than needed for every inch of rows in the edge. If you pick up a stitch every other row, the band will be puckered.

Reference books provide different ratios for picking up stitches along a selvage edge. Some say pick up 3 stitches for every 4 rows and others say 4 stitches for every 5 rows. Both work in most cases,

but if you want to be precise, use the gauge ratios of your project. Using the example above, you must use up 6 horizontal bars for every 8 rows. You should also consider the stitch pattern for the band because it may have a very different gauge than the main fabric. It's always a good idea to work a gauge swatch for the band's stitch pattern to determine the number of stitches per inch for that pattern. If the band is K2, P2 Rib, you may need to pick up more stitches than for a seed stitch or stockinette stitch band. If you save your gauge swatch, you can work a sample band along a vertical edge, trying out different pick-up ratios or different needle sizes before picking up stitches on the garment. This saves time in the long run.

An additional consideration is the multiple of the stitch pattern of the band. For example, if a pattern states that 60 stitches should be picked up along a continuous crew neck of a pullover and the stitch pattern is K1, P1 Rib, more or fewer stitches can be picked up as long as it is an even number of stitches. If an odd number is picked up, the K1, P1 pattern will be disrupted. So bear in mind the "multiple" of the stitch pattern for the band. As long as you pick up a number of stitches that fits the multiple, the band will work. If an additional stitch is needed, you can always compensate by picking up an extra stitch on a vertical edge or at the seams.

Photos 2 and 3 show stitches picked up along two types of necklines—crew and V-neck. Both are continuous bands worked in K1, P1 Rib. For V-neck bands, it is necessary to decrease stitches at the V or the band will flare.

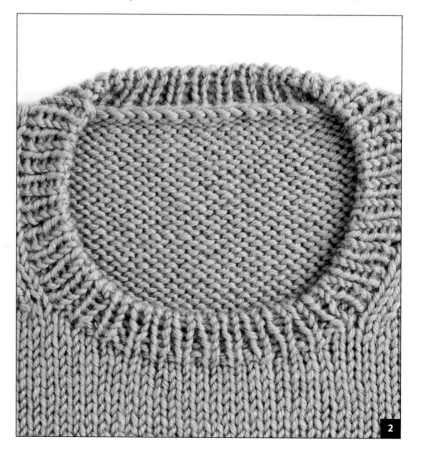

2

In K1, P1 Rib, the best decrease to use is the centered double decrease (S2KP2). Most V-neck patterns with this type of band instruct the knitter to bind off 1 or 3 stitches in the center front. To work this decrease in a V-neck band:

Step 1: Pick up stitches along the neckline. Place markers on either side of the center 3 stitches in the V.

Step 2: Work the first round in K1, P1 Rib to the first marker.

Step 3: Remove the marker. Work the S2KP2 centered double decrease as follows: slip the first 2 stitches together as if you are going to knit them together, knit the third stitch, and then pass the 2 slipped stitches together over the first stitch.

Step 4: Remove the second marker and work in K1, P1 Rib to the end of the round.

Step 5: Work the second round up to the stitch before the center stitch. Work the S2KP2 centered double decrease.

Continue this process until the band is the desired length. Depending on the angle of the V in the neckline, you may want to work the decrease every other round instead of every round. This decrease can also be used for the mitered corner in square necks. ■

Creating the Perfect Pocket

By Colleen Smitherman

Besides serving a practical function, pockets can add visual interest to the overall look of a garment.

Many people like having pockets in their sweaters, especially cardigans. Pockets can be very decorative or unobtrusive, depending on how they are worked. The two most common pocket types are patch pockets and inset pockets. Inset pockets are internal with only the pocket edging, and little or none of the lining showing. Patch pockets are external and are completely visible.

Size and Placement

The opening of a waist-level pocket is at the waist (or a bit lower) with the bottom edge being about 20–22 inches from the shoulder (but always above the lower garment edging), depending on the height of the wearer. The opening of a vertical pocket is usually placed either at the side seam or 1–2 inches in, while the inner edge of a horizontal or angled pocket is usually placed approximately 2–3 inches from the center front.

Pockets on women's garments are about 5–6 inches both wide and deep; longer sweaters and men's garments have larger pockets and cropped jackets and children's garments have smaller pockets. Pockets add weight so they work best on firmly-knit fabric.

The Patch Pocket

Patch pockets can be both functional pockets and design features. They are easy to knit and require little planning; they can be made with just about any yarn, in any stitch pattern and in any shape. If they don't turn out just right, they are easy to remove and replace as shown in Photo 1.

Make and sew on a patch pocket

Plot the area that you would like to place your pocket, and with contrasting waste yarn and a tapestry needle, baste around the area you would like to place your pocket. Determine the number of stitches and rows needed, (based on the gauge of the pocket fabric) and work the pocket, complete with an edging along the opening. Block both the pocket and the main fabric. Sew on the pocket with matching yarn, using mattress stitch (going into 1 bar from the pocket, and then into 1 bar from the main fabric; see the *Construction Essentials* chapter for seaming technique) to join the vertical edges and the invisible horizontal seaming method for the horizontal bottom edge.

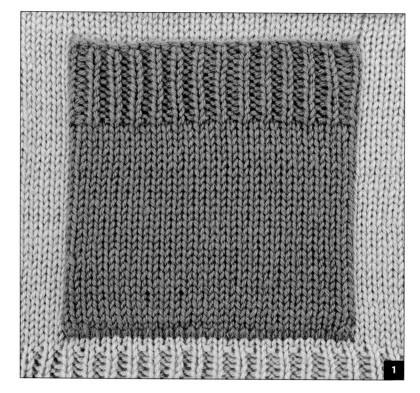

Child's hand-warmer "uni-pocket"

Patch pockets are adaptable to many shapes and sizes.

For the child's hand-warmer "uni-pocket," begin by knitting a few inches of plain stockinette stitch to create depth at the bottom of the pocket. Shape the angled opening by making decreases bordered by K1, P1 Rib as shown in Photo 2. The top will be sewn on so it doesn't need any edge treatment.

Knit-on patch pocket

Patch pockets can also be knit onto your garment. Sew baste lines with contrasting yarn at the pocket boundaries as shown in Photo 3.

At the lower edge, pick up and knit the stitches needed for the pocket from the main fabric, making sure that you are always picking up from the same row. Work a wrong-side row. To attach the pocket at the sides, join on each right-side row as follows: At the beginning of the row, skip one row on the garment fabric and, using the left needle, pick up the outer leg of the corresponding garment stitch, and then knit this leg and the first pocket stitch together; at the end of the row, slip the last stitch to the right needle knitwise, skip one row of the garment fabric and using the left needle, pick up the outer leg of the corresponding garment stitch, slip the pocket stitch back to the left-hand needle and knit the 2 stitches together through the back loops (ssk). Work a wrong side row without attaching.

Inset Pockets

Most inset pockets require some planning before the garment is knit, the exception being the "afterthought" pocket. To decrease bulk, a very flat stitch (such as stockinette stitch) is usually used for pocket linings. Linings are often knit with the same gauge and yarn as the garment; if using a different yarn for the lining, check to be sure that the yarn can be laundered in the same manner, that it is colorfast, and that it won't show through to the right side of the garment, and adjust for gauge as necessary.

The Horizontal Inset Pocket

This style pocket, as shown in Photo 4, is appropriate for garments where you don't want the pocket to compete with other design aspects because only the pocket top shows.

Making the lining and creating an opening

To knit the lining, cast on the stitches needed for the pocket width and work enough rows for the depth minus the depth of the pocket-top edging—if the depth is to be six inches and the top edging will be one inch, the lining should be five inches deep. Place the stitches onto a stitch holder or waste yarn.

Next, begin the garment piece and work the same number of rows as in the lining ending with a wrong side row. On the next row, knit to the pocket location, slip the garment stitches where the pocket is to be to a piece of waste yarn, and then slip the lining stitches onto the needle in their place as shown in Photo 5. Continue to work the garment piece on these stitches.

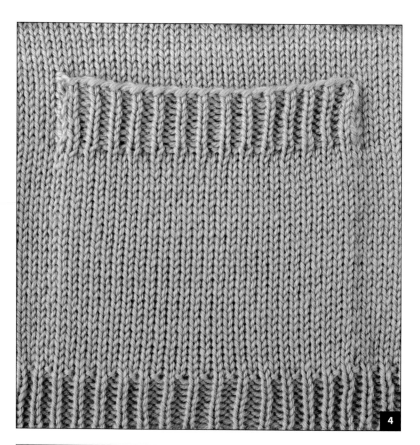

Complete the pocket top edging

When the garment piece is complete, slip the garment stitches—which are on hold on waste yarn—onto needles as shown in Photo 6, and work the pocket top edging. Sew the sides of the edging to the front side of the garment

Sew the lining on the inside

As shown in Photo 7, sew basting guidelines with contrasting yarn on the inside for seaming the lining. Sew the lining in place with yarn that matches the garment, taking care to avoid having the stitches show on the right side.

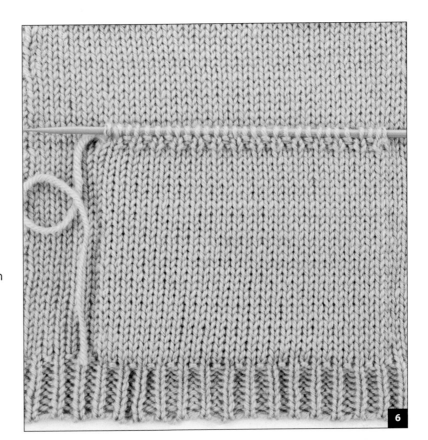

6

7

The Afterthought Inset Pocket

An afterthought inset pocket looks identical to a horizontal inset pocket, but it allows the placement of an inset pocket after a garment is complete.

Prepare the opening

To create an opening for the pocket, decide the location and mark the outside boundaries, as shown by blue yarn markers in Photo 8. Identify the row for the opening by deciding the depth of the pocket minus the height that will be added by the pocket edging, and then snip the side of a stitch in the middle of the row. With a crochet hook, tease the yarn out of the row, working in one direction and picking up the live stitches above and below with two yarn needles threaded with waste yarn. When you reach one boundary, thread the other ends of the waste yarn with the yarn needles and work to the other side. If a stitch happens to drop, knit it back with the crochet hook.

Knit the pocket lining

For the lining, slip the stitches from the top of the opening to a knitting needle, being careful not to twist them as shown in Photo 9; work the lining down to the desired depth.

Knit a pocket edging on the stitches from the bottom of the opening, and complete the pocket in the same manner as for the horizontal inset pocket.

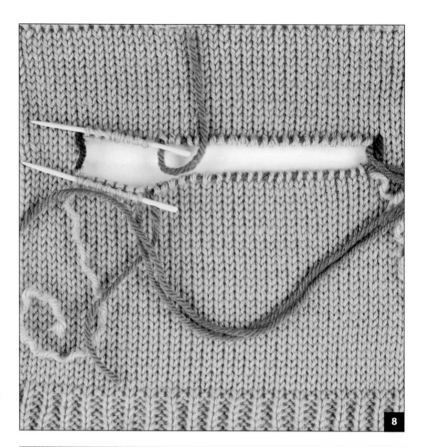

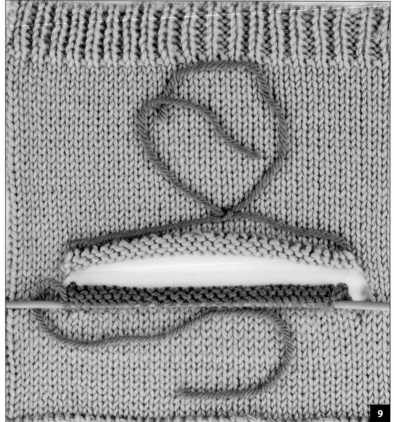

The Vertical Inset Pocket

This is a good choice for garments with vertical elements, such as cables, because the pocket can be worked between them. The example in Photo 10 has a left-side opening (as worn); reverse the instructions for a right-side opening.

Create the pocket opening and knit the pocket lining and first section.

Work the garment piece to the position where you want the bottom edge of the pocket lining, ending with a wrong side row. On the next row, knit to the spot where you want the pocket opening and put the remaining stitches on hold; they will be used for the other side of the main garment fabric. Loosely cast on the lining stitches (shown in Photo 11, using contrasting yarn).

10

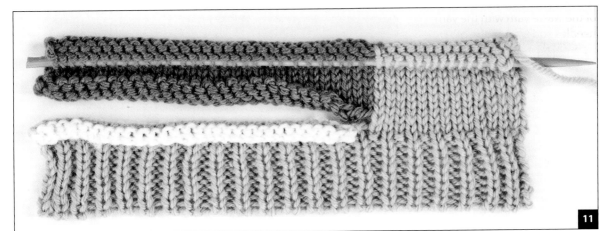

11

Working the side edge in the garment's pattern stitch and the lining stitches in stockinette stitch, work to the desired depth of pocket, ending with a wrong side row.

If working a more complex main pattern stitch, put the side stitches on hold and, using a separate length of yarn, bind off the lining stitches. If working in stockinette stitch, put all the stitches on hold.

Knit the second section and rejoin the sections

Slip the stitches for the other side onto a needle and add a selvage stitch at the opening edge. Work the same number of rows in the project's stitch pattern, ending on a wrong side row, as shown in Photo 12.

If you've bound off the top lining edge, slip the first section back to the needle and, using a single ball of yarn, join by working across both sides, eliminating the selvage stitch at the opening edge.

If you've left the lining stitches on hold, slip the side edge and lining stitches to another needle. With the lining stitches behind the main garment stitches, knit across the side stitches, and then fuse the lining and the main fabric by knitting one stitch from the main fabric together with one lining stitch; work to the end of the row. Continue working the garment piece.

For the edging, pick up and knit stitches along the pocket edge. On the second row, add a selvage stitch on each side. Work the desired edging, and then mattress stitch the edging in place from the right side. Complete the pocket on the inside in the same manner as for the horizontal inset pocket.

12

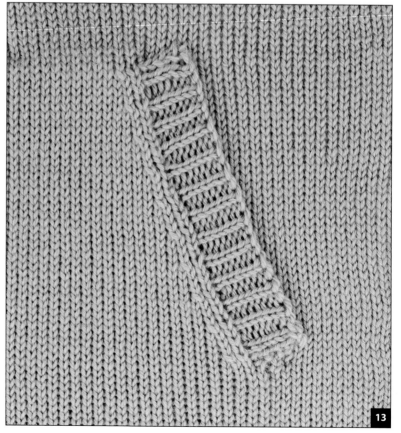

13

For a double/folded pocket lining (not shown), cast on twice the number of stitches needed for the pocket width when knitting the first section. Fold the lining in half, seam the free side to the corresponding location on the second section, seam the sides together, and sew to the inside.

The Angled Inset Pocket

This is a great style for sporty garments. Use the same yarn for the lining and the garment because some of the lining will be visible. The sample in Photo 13 has a left-side opening (as worn); reverse the instructions for a right-side opening.

Begin the lining, create the pocket opening and insert the lining

The bottom edge of the lining of this type of pocket usually falls below the pocket opening, so the lining is started first. Cast on the number of stitches needed for the lining width and work enough rows for the extra depth, ending on a wrong side row. Move the stitches onto waste yarn.

Work the garment piece to the point where you want the lower edge of the pocket opening, ending on a wrong side row; this will be at least the same number of rows above the lower edging as you have already worked for the lining. On the next row, work to the spot where you want the pocket opening and put the remaining stitches on hold; they will be used for the other side of the main garment fabric. Slip the lining stitches onto the working needle and work across, joining them to the side edge, as shown in Photo 14. Continue to work the section with lining stitches until the desired height of the pocket is reached, ending on a wrong-side row. Move the stitches to waste yarn.

Knit the second section, shaping the opening, and rejoin the sections

Slip the stitches for the second section onto needles and work

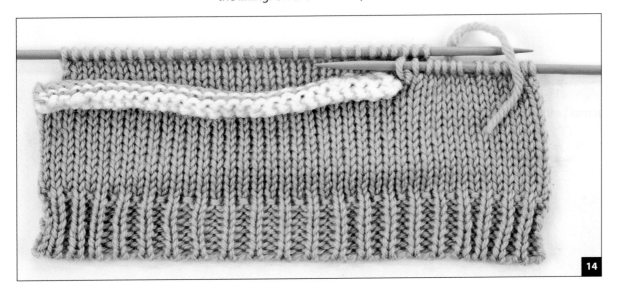

14

the same number of rows as the first section, ending on a wrong side row, and at the same time make evenly spaced decreases one or more stitches from the edge of the opening—working the decreases every 4 rows makes a nice slant. Count the number of stitches left on the needle after shaping, and with a separate ball of yarn, bind off the same number of corresponding stitches on the pocket lining extension. Rejoin both sections and finish the piece as shown in Photo 15.

For the edging, pick up stitches along the pocket edge, work an edging with selvage stitches on each side, and then sew the edging in place on the right side, following the Invisible Vertical to Horizontal seaming instructions on page 40. Complete the pocket on the inside in the same manner as for the horizontal inset pocket. ■

15

A good way to preview what a pocket might look like is to cut out trial pockets from paper or fabric and pin them onto a comparable garment.

If you are not sure if you have enough yarn for pockets, knit the sweater, and then add afterthought pockets. It will only take a small amount for the pocket edging, and if necessary, you can use a comparable yarn for the linings.

It is easy to slip a pocket into a side seam. Knit a lining of the desired depth and twice the desired width. Open the side seam (if necessary), sew the lining sides to the front and back edge stitches with the flattest seam possible, sew the lining sides together, and secure to the inside of the garment front.

Leave extra-long yarn tails when knitting linings, edgings or patch pockets so they can be used for seaming. Always sew the bottoms of pockets securely to prevent items from slipping out of them. Although pockets are often sewn in with

yarn, using thread might be a better choice in some situations.

Linings which won't be seen can be flattened to reduce bulk by steaming them with an iron, and then letting them dry with a heavy object on top.

Pocket tops that have sagged can often be tightened up attractively with a row of crochet followed by an optional row of reverse crochet.

There are many options for pocket edgings, such as two-color ribbing, garter stitch, seed stitch and/or lace. Edgings can be decorated with buttons, beads, novelty yarns or cables sewn on horizontally. (See the Enticing Embellishments chapter) Always include a selvage stitch on each side of the edging; it will disappear when the edging is sewn to the main fabric.

Pocket edgings on vertical and angled pockets can be created as you work the second section by incorporating edging stitches into the appropriate locations.

Tailored Elements:
Hems & Facings

By Jodi Lewanda

Hems add strength and integrity to a finished garment, as well as providing a neat and professional look.

In certain cases, a hem can be a crucial component in the construction of a garment. A hem will hold an edge in place, keep it flat and give the lower edge of the garment additional weight and a neat, finished look.

There are a few things to bear in mind when knitting a hem: A crisp turning edge is desirable for neatness; a hem will add bulk so you should find ways to minimize that; the inside hem of a tube should have a smaller circumference than the outer fabric; the hem should be joined to the main fabric in such a way that the join is as elastic as the rest of the fabric.

Turning Edges

There are a few ways to incorporate a hem folding line into your knitting.

Purl ridge

The simplest way to work a turning ridge is to work a row of purl stitches on the right side, as shown in Photo 1. This kind of hem creates a natural folding line, as pictured in Photo 2.

Picot edge

The most decorative turning edge is a picot edge. When you're ready to begin your seam, work on a right side row as follows: K1 (selvage stitch), *yo, k2tog; repeat from * to the last stitch, k1 (selvage stitch). The Photo 3 example illustrates how this type of seam looks open, and Photo 4, hemmed. If working in the round, work [yo, k2tog] around.

3

4

Slip-stitch ridge

A third option is a slip-stitch horizontal turning ridge. If worked on a piece that will be seamed, maintain selvage stitches and work a right side row as follows: [K1, sl 1 with yarn in front] across, as shown in the Photo 5 example. The natural folding properties of this row are much more subtle than either the purl ridge or the picot turn, as shown in Photo 6, making the other two methods preferable.

Joining the Hem

There are also several ways to join the lower edge of the hem to the main fabric. The keys are to retain elasticity across the join and to keep it from being visible on the right side of the fabric.

Knit together

The version that is both elastic and invisible is the "knit-together" join. To work this join, begin the piece with either a provisional cast-on or a long-tail cast-on. Work in stockinette stitch to the turning ridge, work the turning ridge as desired, and then work the main fabric to the same depth as the hem facing. Now, either unzip the provisional cast-on and put the live stitches on a smaller needle, or use a smaller needle to catch the bottom strand of each cast-on stitch, if you've done a long-tail cast-on. Folding the fabric along the turning ridge, hold the two needles parallel (working needle in front) with the wrong sides of the fabric together, as Photo 7 demonstrates. Knit the first stitch of the main fabric together with the first stitch of the hem facing, and then continue across working k2tog in this manner. The hem will be joined and you can continue knitting the rest of the body. Photo 8, shows the completed hem, shown from the wrong side.

This join is most successful if worked on smaller pieces, such as the tops of socks, sleeve cuffs or mitten cuffs. The greater the circumference of the garment piece being hemmed (i.e. lower edge of a sweater), the more this join has a tendency to "flip" at the join line. If that's the case, you might find one of the following joins better.

Grafting stitches

Another way of joining the live stitches of a hem to the main fabric is to graft the live stitches to the wrong side of the main fabric using a basic Kitchener stitch, page 42. This will work whether you are working the hem from the bottom (having started with a provisional cast-on) or are working a top-down garment and are ending with live stitches. When grafting into the main fabric, just follow the pathway of the purl stitches.

Sewn edge

Lastly, you can sew the edge of the hem to the main fabric, stitch for stitch, using a whipstitch motion as shown in Photo 9. If working from the bottom-up, you can either sew from live stitches (having started with a provisional cast-on) or from the outer edge of a long-tail cast-on. To make the sewing line much less visible on the right side, you can use a sharp needle to pierce the purl head of the stitch on the main fabric side instead of using a blunt needle to catch the entire strand of the purl head. Experiment on a swatch and decide which method you like best. Make sure that you are sewing stitches together that are in the same column of stitches—you don't want the hem to skew. Spread the fabric a bit while sewing so that the sewing line remains elastic.

Minimizing Bulk of Hem Facing

Since any turned hem adds a second layer of fabric, it's important to minimize the extra bulk and prevent the hem from splaying. This can be achieved in a number of ways.

Smaller needle size

Work the hem facing on needles that are 13 sizes smaller than the main fabric needle. This will give the fabric of the inner facing a smaller circumference than the main fabric and will prevent splay. Switch to the main needle size after the turning row/round.

One downside to this method is that using smaller needles for the facing makes the facing fabric denser. Since sometimes this is undesirable, what are other options?

Fewer stitches

Work the hem facing with 510 percent fewer stitches, but on same-size needle as main fabric. Increase the number of stitches to the full number 1 or 2 rows before the turning row. When joining the hem facing to the main fabric, skip a main fabric stitch every 10 or 20 stitches, whether using the knit-together join, grafting or sewing.

Lighter-weight yarn

Work the hem facing with a lighter-weight yarn, but use the same size needles as the main fabric. Change to the main yarn 1 or 2 rows before the turning row. Using a lighter-weight yarn will decrease the bulk of the facing while allowing you to keep the stitch count constant. It is not critical that the hem facing yarn be the same color as the main yarn because it won't show. However, if you want them to be the same, strip out a ply of a multiple-plied main yarn and use that for the facing yarn.

9

Vertical Facings

Facings can also be worked along vertical edges of fabric, including along button bands or zipper openings. As with hems, they are also used for edge strength, shape and weight. Facings are usually decorative so that when the garment's edge is turned back, there is added detail. The concepts are similar, but there are fewer problems to solve than with horizontal facings; for example, fabric splay is not usually a problem along a vertical edge.

To prepare a vertical facing, cast on enough stitches for the main fabric, adding extra stitches for the facing plus 1 extra stitch for the turning edge.

Turning edge

Slip stitch edge

The cleanest turning edge for a vertical facing is made by slipping the turning edge stitch every other row—the facing will naturally turn back along this line as shown in Photos 10 and 11.

Garter stitch edge

Another option is to work the
turning edge stitch in garter stitch
(knit every row). This does not
make as sharp a turning edge as
with the slipped stitch, but can
be fairly decorative as shown in
Photos 12 and 13.

Corner Facings

A mitered corner facing consists of a horizontal hem and a vertical hem.

Before beginning, decide how many rows (horizontal) and stitches wide (vertical) the facings will be. Referring to Photos 14 and 15, and starting with the horizontal hem, cast on the final width of stitches, minus half of the row count of the facing. For example, if the facing is to be 10 rows, cast on the final piece's width, minus 5 stitches.

Work the horizontal facing, increasing 1 stitch at mitered corner end of row, every other row.

When the horizontal facing is complete, work a turning row. Add one stitch for the vertical turning column and continue increasing at the mitered corner end of row, every other row until the vertical facing reaches the desired width, then work without additional increases. Remember to continue making a turning stitch between the main piece and the vertical hem.

Turn the facings to the inside (wrong side) and sew them to the main piece. Finally, sew the diagonal corner where the horizontal and vertical hems meet.

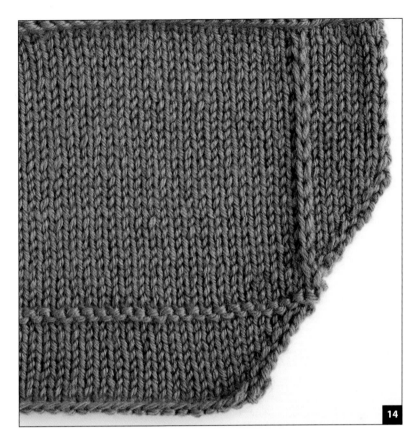

14

15

Facings can be made with the same yarn, same color or with the same yarn, different color, as shown in Photo 16.

Since some colors cause the yarn to have slightly different properties, the facing yarn should be swatched for gauge and the stitch count adjusted if necessary to match the size of the garment's gauge swatch.

As the Photo 17 example shows, facings can be completed in a different stitch pattern from the main body of the garment. If this technique is used, gauge must be determined for each facing layer and adjusted.

Final Thoughts

Facings can be produced with a different yarn from the main body of the garment. The yarns used can be of different textures, fibers, etc. Again, gauge swatches for the facing should be completed to ensure that the facings will not be too large or too small.

Decorative facings are perfect for folded-back collars, cuffs and pocket flaps. Even if the facing is not meant to show permanently, it adds a bit of fun detail.

Although facings are meant to give extra support to a garment, have fun with them. Use different yarns, stitches and sewing techniques to add a little interest to the inside of your garment. ■

16

17

The ABCs of Buttonholes

By Arenda Holladay

Choosing the right buttonhole will add functionality and stylish flair to your finished garment.

Buttonholes are the reason many knitters make only pullovers. Evenly spaced, neat and tidy buttonholes that don't stretch out and suit the stitch pattern of the band can be tricky to make. Most patterns do not specify the type of buttonhole construction, so it is up to the knitter. Some general rules apply to any type of buttonhole you select.

General Rules

1. Select the buttons before making the buttonholes. It is easier to make a buttonhole fit a button than to find a button that will fit the buttonhole.

2. Pick up the stitches for the band properly. Use the spaces between the horizontal bars between the selvage stitch and the first stitch. (These are the same bars you would use for a mattress stitch seam.) This provides support for the bands. Use an appropriate ratio when picking up the stitches, picking up 4 stitches for every 5 rows works for most stitch patterns.

3. Select the type of buttonhole which best suits the type of

band (1x1 rib, 2x2 rib, seed stitch, etc.) and the type of fiber. For example, an eyelet buttonhole in ribbing worked in mohair would be very difficult to see (and find).

4. Knit a test swatch or use your gauge swatch to see which type of buttonhole you want to use before knitting the button and buttonhole bands. You can try different types of buttonholes and determine the best spacing. It will save you time in the long run.

5. Knit the buttonband first. You can use it to determine spacing for the buttonholes. Traditionally, for women's garments this is the left side; for men's, the right.

Placing Buttonholes

Buttonholes should be evenly placed along the band. Generally, the first and last buttonholes are placed ½ to 1 inch from the top and bottom. The remaining buttonholes are evenly spaced between them. Use the buttonband to determine the placement. Some knitters measure

while others count rows. Counting rows will give you more accurate results, but whichever method you use, you must take into consideration how many rows it takes to make the buttonhole. For example, a simple eyelet buttonhole requires only one row to make. Buttonholes should also be centered in the band. Leave at least 3 stitches or 4 rows from the edge before starting the buttonhole.

Types of Buttonholes

There are four basic types of buttonholes: eyelet, vertical, horizontal and loop.

Eyelet buttonhole

The eyelet buttonhole is almost invisible and can be used almost everywhere. It works well with all types of yarns and can be worked into all stitch patterns. The simplest version takes only one row to make. The drawback is that it is small and prone to snagging. Sometimes it can be difficult to find this buttonhole on a finished garment.

To make an eyelet buttonhole: Knit 2 stitches together and make a yarn over (k2tog, yo).

Photo 1 shows eyelets worked in 2 stitch patterns, stockinette stitch and seed stitch. It is very difficult to see the buttonhole in the seed stitch.

If you are working in ribbing, the buttonhole will look better if you make the yarn over a purl stitch. There are two ways you can do this. Work to the knit stitch before the purl where you want the buttonhole. Work an ssk decrease using the knit and purl stitch, and then make the yarn over. You can also work to the purl stitch where you want the buttonhole. Make a yarn over, and then work a k2tog decrease using the purl and knit stitch after the yarn over. Photo 2 shows the ssk version of this kind of buttonhole.

Vertical buttonhole

The vertical buttonhole is almost invisible when worked in ribbing, but it can be worked in any stitch pattern. It is very easy to work. The drawback with this type of buttonhole is that it can stretch out of shape. In addition, since each side of the buttonhole is worked independently, it is necessary to weave in two yarn tails for each buttonhole.

To make a vertical buttonhole:
Step 1: Knit to the position of the buttonhole and drop main ball of yarn.

Step 2: Attach a second ball of yarn, leaving at least a 6-inch yarn tail, and knit across the row.

Step 3: Work each side of the buttonhole independently.

Step 4: When the buttonhole is the desired length, rejoin the

two pieces by knitting across the row with the main ball of yarn.

Step 5: Cut the second ball of yarn, leaving at least a 6-inch yarn tail.

Step 6: When all the buttonholes are complete, weave in the yarn tails, reinforcing the top and bottom of each buttonhole.

Photo 3 shows two buttonholes: One with a different colored yarn used for the second ball of yarn and the yarn tails not yet woven in, and a completed buttonhole in one color.

Horizontal buttonhole

There are two ways to work horizontal buttonholes. The first one is worked in two rows. In the first row, you bind off the stitches for the buttonhole, and in the second row, you cast on (using either the backwards loop or knitted cast-on) the same number of stitches over the buttonhole. The problem with this method is that it is not very neat. The bound-off and cast-on edges do not match.

The one-row version of the horizontal buttonhole is preferable to the two-row version because it is much neater; it is also the sturdiest of all buttonholes

and does not need additional reinforcement.

To work a one-row horizontal buttonhole:

Step 1: Work to buttonhole location.

Step 2: Bring yarn forward and slip the first stitch on the left needle purlwise.

Step 3: Bring the yarn to the back.

Step 4: Slip the next stitch on the left needle purlwise to the right needle.

Step 5: Pass the second slipped stitch on the right needle over the first stitch (as if to bind off).

Repeat Steps 4 and 5 until the buttonhole is the right size.

Step 6: Slip the last bound-off stitch to the left needle.

Step 7: Turn the work and use the cable cast-on method to cast on one more stitch than you bound off. (When you work the cable cast-on, if you insert the needle purlwise instead of knitwise between the stitches, the top edge will better match the bottom edge of the buttonhole.)

Step 8: Turn the work.

Step 9: Slip the first stitch on the left needle to the right needle and pass the extra cast-on stitch over the slipped stitch. Work the remaining stitches on the needle.

Photo 4 shows the horizontal buttonhole. The knitwise cable cast-on was used for the bottom buttonhole and the purlwise cable cast-on was used for the top buttonhole.

Loop buttonholes

This type of buttonhole is worked on the edge of the work. Loop buttonholes are strong, attractive and can accommodate any size button, but they work best with a button with a shank. The most common type of loop buttonhole is the I-cord. It can be worked at the same time as the band or made separately and added later. If you can crochet, loops can also be crocheted to the piece.

I-cord loop

I-cord loops are generally worked as part of an attached I-cord band. Attached I-cord bands are discussed in Bands, Borders and Ribbings, page 94. The basic procedure for an attached I-cord band is to slip the last I-cord stitch knitwise, knit up a stitch from the selvage, and then pass the slipped I-cord stitch over that stitch.

4

To make an I-cord loop buttonhole:

Step 1: Work to the location for the buttonhole. Knit all the I-cord stitches; do not slip the last stitch or knit up a stitch from the selvage.

Step 2: Slip the I-cord stitches purlwise back to the left needle.

Repeat these steps until the I-cord buttonhole is the desired length. Resume working the attached I-cord until you reach the location for the next buttonhole.

Photos 5 and 6 show two approaches to the I-cord loop. In Photo 5, a loop is made by attaching the I-cord to the same location on the selvage. In Photo 6, the loop is stretched along the selvage and then attached further along the selvage, which produces a more traditional buttonhole.

Another way to use I-cords for a buttonhole is to knit a long I-cord independently. This I-cord can then be shaped into a frog closure and sewn to the garment. Photo 7 shows this type of butttonhole.

Crocheted loop

This type of loop is added after the piece is complete and the bands have been worked. This buttonhole works well for garments worked in a stitch pattern, like garter stitch, where bands are not necessary. Photo 8 shows a crocheted loop on garter stitch.

To make a crocheted loop buttonhole:

Step 1: With a crochet hook, pull a loop through from the WS to the RS at the location for the top end of the buttonhole.

Step 2: Crochet a chain the desired length for the buttonhole.

Step 3: Remove the loop from the crochet hook and insert the hook at the bottom end of the buttonhole from the WS to the RS. Pull the loop through.

Step 4: Turn the work and chain one stitch to lock the loop in place.

Step 5: Work single crochet stitches over the chain to the other side. Use a slip stitch to lock it in place. Cut the yarn and weave in all yarn tails.

Before working the buttonholes on the actual garment, experiment with a few different types on a swatch. It's much easier to perfect your technique on a swatch than on a garment front. This will enable you to select the buttonhole which best suits the yarn, buttons and, ultimately, the garment. ∎

7

8

The Wonderful World of Working With Zippers

By Leslye Solomon

Today, the zipper is everywhere—in clothing, tents, upholstery, luggage, leather goods and, of course, commercial and hand-made sweaters. Installing a zipper can be a very easy task if you follow these next few pages.

Imagine how fascinating it would have been to see the first airplane fly, the first electric light bulb glow and how the first zipper brought together two pieces of a garment. It's an invention that took about 80 years to accept.

After a slow birth and years of rejection, the zipper finally found its way into everything from slacks, suitcases and even space suits. The zippers used today, however, are a little different than the original invention.

The evolution of the zipper fell into the hands of Whitcomb L. Judson who, being fascinated by gadgets and devices, patented the first zipper-like design in 1891. By 1905, zippers were being utilized; however, they weren't considered "practical." The design used today, based on interlocking teeth, was an improvement developed by an employee of Whitcomb Judson's— Swedish born scientist, Gideon Sundback. Originally patented as the "Hookless Fastener", the zipper was further improved and patented again in 1917 as the "Separable Fastener". Only after Sundbach had remodeled Judson's fastener into a more streamlined and reliable form was the fastener a success.

B. F. Goodrich Company made zippers popular by using them in galoshes. One of its first customers was the U.S. Army. It applied zippers to the clothing and gear of the troops of World War I. These new galoshes could be fastened with a single zip of the hand. A Goodrich executive is said to have slid the fastener up and down on the boot and exclaimed, "Zip 'er up," echoing the sound made by this almost magical device. Henceforth, the fasteners were called "zippers."

Selecting Zippers for Sweaters

There are two types of zippers that are most often used for sweaters: the separating zipper and the conventional zipper. The separating zipper un-zips into two pieces and is used most frequently for cardigans. The conventional zipper opens at one end and is appropriate for garments which are fitted on the body. Imagine this shorter type of zipper at the back of the neck or the top of a skirt, which, when unzipped, would allow one to wear a closely fit garment when the zipper is closed. This kind of zipper could be a decorative

application at the bottom of a V-neck, at the cuffs or at the back bottom edge of a sweater, perhaps acting as a vent. Use this application for pocket openings; however, both ends would require self-made stoppers. While selecting the correct length and color of your desired zipper, do not forget to verify the type of zipper (separating or conventional) on the package before making a purchase.

Most often a zipper needs to be installed so that it is invisible and neatly sewn into the fabric. On the other hand, some zippers make a fashion statement. The tapes and teeth are decorative and are intended to be visible. There are beautiful color combinations such as black paired with white, yellow with green or blue with pink. Make your own combination by taking two colors and pairing them with other colors. You may find the zipper is made with elegant tapes of luxurious fabrics, such as white or black satin and silver, gold or bronze metallic. From a rainbow of colors of teeth to a zipper of Austrian Crystals, the discovery of the perfect zipper, like a group of exciting buttons, might spark your next sweater idea. Purchase a zipper that is at least two inches longer than the intended length, as it is easy to shorten the zipper to the exact length required.

Unusual Applications

You don't have to limit zippers to just opening and closing a garment. Zippers can be used as non-functional decorations. You can use a zipper to decorate a neck edge, line the bottom edge of a sleeve and decorate around the opening edge of a hood. The teeth of the zipper offer a fashionable decoration, allowing you to ignite your imagination while keeping in mind that there are no rules.

Parts of the Zipper

It is a good idea to be able to officially identify the parts of a zipper.

The components of a zipper are shown in Photo 1.

The typical zipper consists of two strips of twill-type fabric tape, each affixed to one of the two pieces to be joined, carrying many specially shaped metal or plastic teeth. The slider, operated by hand, moves along the rows of teeth. Inside the slider is a Y-shaped channel that meshes together or separates the opposing rows of teeth, depending on the direction of its movement. As the slide is moved upward, two rows of teeth merge and interlock.

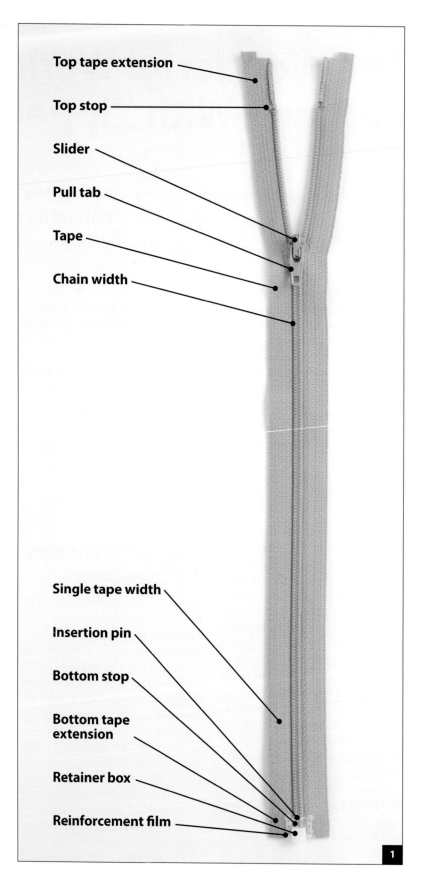

Top tape extension
Top stop
Slider
Pull tab
Tape
Chain width

Single tape width
Insertion pin
Bottom stop
Bottom tape extension
Retainer box
Reinforcement film

1

Prepare Your Garment

The following method utilizes a single crochet edge followed by a backwards single crochet, which is applied to the edge of your finished garment. This edge creates an almost-raised, piped edge. Most important is the line between the two rows of crochet, which becomes your sewing guide when sewing the zipper in place. Utilizing a sewing machine will make the sewing of the zipper very secure and strong. There's no need to worry if a sewing machine is not available; small backstitching by hand is more time-consuming, but it is also a viable option.

After your garment is complete, block your pieces using your favorite blocking method. Block your pieces to the shape intended, but encourage the fabric to drape, imitating what gravity will eventually do. When all pieces are the width and length intended, prepare the garment as follows by finishing the edge where the zipper will be sewn.

Using a crochet hook of an appropriate size for your yarn, with the right side facing and working from right to left, single crochet as described below in every other row along the edge. Be consistent when inserting the hook. The slightest change may create a noticeable imperfection. Make sure that you consistently insert the crochet hook along the edge, one whole stitch in from the edge. Do not split the edge stitch. It is helpful to work on a flat surface. Your single crochet should lay flat and not exhibit a curve, which would indicate that too many stitches are along the edge. You can control the size of the final loop while crocheting; therefore, watch how the crochet performs as it is being applied.

Note: The crochet instructions that follow are for right-handed people; if you are left-handed, work the crochet edgings in the opposite directions with single crochet going left-to-right and the backwards single crochet going right-to-left.

Single crochet: As shown in Photo 2, place a slip knot on hook. Beginning at the right-hand corner, insert the hook through the edge, one stitch in from the edge. Yarn over and bring the yarn over through the edge. Two loops will be on the hook. Yarn over again and bring the yarn over through the two loops. Skip the next row and repeat. Continue along for the length of the edge. When you have reached the end, chain one and do not turn.

Backwards single crochet: When the entire edge has been single crocheted, begin working "backwards" from left to right as shown in Photo 3. With the last loop still on the hook, insert the hook through the single crochet chain stitch just completed. Reach back and yarn over and bring the loop through the edge. Then yarn over and bring the yarn over through the two loops. Continue working from left to right, inserting the hook under the next

single crochet chain. The view of the hook almost disappears, as it is somewhat behind the fabric. Continue this process to the end. Cut the yarn, leaving a 10- to 12-inch tail to be woven in later, and bring the end of the yarn through the final loop. Repeat on the other side of the garment.

Steam the two edges so they lay flat and straight. The edge creates a sharp right angle from the bottom. Allow the steamed edges to set and dry for many hours before continuing to work.

Position & Baste Zipper

As shown in the Photo 4 example, gently steam the zipper to remove any folds or creases from when it was packaged.

Using a sewing needle and color of thread that matches the garment, position the zipper in place, with top edge of the zipper extending above the opening. Using a few pins, position it in place, having the outer edge of the backwards single crochet either hiding the teeth as shown in Photo 5, or decoratively exposing them. Let the top of the zipper with the slider extend beyond the top.

Loosely sew or baste in place, making large, and possibly temporary, running stitches and having the teeth of the zipper slightly hidden along the edge of the backwards single crochet. Remember that the pull-tab will have to have some space to hide under the crochet. Be careful not to position the zipper so close that it will get caught in the yarn of the crochet. The outside edge of the crochet will be placed along the center of the zipper teeth.

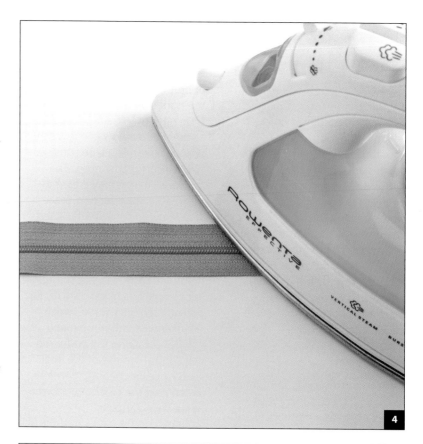

If you want the elements of the zipper to show, position the crochet edge so that the zipper is exposed. After securely basting in place, stitch as shown in Photo 5. Make sure you are completely satisfied with your preliminary hand stitching and correct any imperfection at this point by re-basting if necessary. The basting stitches will securely hold the zipper in place for the next step.

Option One: Sewing Machine Method

As shown in Photo 6, position the zipper foot of your sewing machine in order to sew one side of the zipper. Selecting a relatively large stitch size, stitch the zipper to the sweater following the line that is between the two rows of crochet. With the slider temporarily positioned above, it will be easier to sew with the machine since the foot will not have to maneuver around it. The pull-tab will be out of the sewing line. Securely stitch and backstitch the beginning of each seam. Repeat on the other side. Make sure that the tape underneath is completely included in the stitching line.

Option Two: Sewing by Hand

Thread a sewing needle and back stitch along the line between the two lines of crochet as demonstrated in Photo 7. Try to make your stitches close together and firm. Your stitching should be invisible and buried in the line.

Secure all ends of thread. Remove any obvious, large basting stitches as shown in Photo 8 by looking on underside of zipper as well as the right side. Leave any basting stitches that are hidden or caught in the stitching as they may be too difficult to remove and are not noticeable.

Adjust the Length of Zipper

Pull the zipper pull-tab down to center of zipper. With the zigzag stitch of your machine adjusted to not move fabric, make a strong zipper stopper at each edge of top of zipper, just under the top edge.

If you are not using a sewing machine, using matching sewing thread and a sewing needle, sew a stitch repeatedly in one place as shown in Photo 9 to create your stopper even with, or slightly below, top of garment. Cut the zipper tape above the stopper, as shown in Photo 10.

With proper zipper installation, you will enjoy a secure and sealed closure for your sweaters for years. With every new zipper installed by you, you'll soon realize how easy, convenient and stylish it is to include a zipper in your next project. ■

Finishing Details: "The Extras"

Learn how you can add a little glitz to your finished garments and accessories. In The Art of Short Rows, Jean Clement shows you how you can add short rows to shape your garments in some new and unexpected ways. Myra Wood opens up a world of innovative edgings, embroidery and beading techniques in Enticing Embellishments.

Decorative Details: Bands, Borders & Ribbing

By Jodi Lewanda

Bands, borders and ribbing can provide strength and visual appeal to your finished projects.

Bands

A band is the functional edge of a knitted piece and is used to keep the edge from curling, give the piece strength and provide visual interest.

Although a band can be worked in many stitch patterns, one of its most important purposes is to keep the edge of the main fabric from curling; so, usually non-curling, "flat" stitches are used. Bands are most commonly worked in garter stitch, seed stitch and various ribbings, all of which are non-curling patterns. Remember that these stitch patterns will have different gauges than the primary fabric—some contract (ribs), while others spread out (garter stitch); if necessary, use a different size needle than your main needle (usually smaller) or work the lower band with fewer/more stitches than the rest of the garment.

As shown in Photo 1, a **garter stitch** band is worked by knitting every row until the band is the desired height, and then switching to the main body stitch, adjusting the stitch count as necessary on the transition row.

Seed stitch is a pebbly stitch, as Photo 2 shows, and is worked as a k1, p1, repeat. If there is an odd number of band stitches, each row begins with a knit stitch whereas if there is an even number of stitches, each row alternates, the first row starting with a knit stitch, the second row starting with a purl stitch. The key thing to remember is to knit the purl stitches and purl the knit stitches as they present themselves.

As shown in Photo 3, **ribbing** is a combination of knit and purl stitches that are aligned vertically on top of each other; simply knit the knit stitches and purl the purl stitches as they present themselves.

2

3

If you want a **curled edge**, as pictured in Photo 4, you can work a band in stockinette stitch. If you use knitting needles one or two sizes smaller than you plan to use for the body fabric, the band will curl more tightly and will help control the lower edge.

Knit vertical bands

As Photo 5 demonstrates, vertical bands can be knitted at the same time as the main fabric, but the row gauge of both fabrics should be the same to prevent distortion at the edge. If the main fabric is stockinette stitch, a seed stitch band will work well.

The width of the vertical band can be equal to, narrower or wider than the bottom or horizontal band. To ensure visually pleasing bands, take the time before starting the project to make a swatch using the desired band stitch. Use this swatch to determine how many rows to work the horizontal edge and how many stitches wide to work the vertical edge.

4

5

Sewn vertical bands

Vertical edge bands can also be made separately from the body fabric and then sewn on. When using this method, make sure the band is just slightly shorter (so that it can be stretched) than the piece it is to be sewn to—this will keep the band from puckering or splaying. Referring to Photo 6, an easy way to do this is to work the band with the same number of rows as the main fabric, but on smaller needles so that you have a shorter row gauge. Then the band can be mattress-stitched to the main fabric, row for row. Remember to always include a selvage stitch at the edge that will be seamed—it will disappear into the seam.

Borders

A border is a decorative band. While borders can be worked using basic band stitches, they can also incorporate ruffles, points, cables, lace panels or just about anything that your heart desires as long as it lies flat.

Some borders can be worked first, then transition directly into the main body of the piece.

Ruffle

In this example, Photo 7 shows a ruffle that is made by casting on twice the number of stitches needed for the actual body piece. Start with a few rows of garter stitch or any other non-rolling stitch, and then work the ruffle to its desired length. On the next right side row, k2tog across. Continue in the body pattern.

Points

In the Photo 8 example, a fun "pointy" border is made to add interest to the bottom of the garment. Each point is made separately, with the last row of stitches being kept on hold. After all the points are complete, they are joined together by working a row across the top of all the points. The number of points multiplied by the number of stitches on the last row of each point divided by the stitch gauge of the pattern in which you are working the point (here, it's garter stitch) should equal the width of the main body fabric, so do the math and adjust the point size before starting.

To make these garter stitch points, cast on 2 stitches, turn; k1, then knit in the front and back of the second stitch. In the next and all following point rows, knit the first stitch, increase in the second stitch as before, then knit to the end of the row. Continue until the point is the desired length and width, and cut the yarn, leaving the point on the needle. Make as many points as you need to match the width of your body fabric. Then, with all the points lined up across your needle, purl a right side row across all the points to join them; note that if the stitch gauge of the main fabric is different from the stitch gauge of the garter points, you may need to increase or decrease stitches on this row so that you have the correct number of stitches for the desired width of the main fabric.

Cable

Other borders can be added on after the main piece is completed. Just about any stitch pattern can be used and sewn to an edge.

To add a cable to the bottom of your garment, first complete the garment. Measure across the bottom of the piece to which the cable will be sewn and make

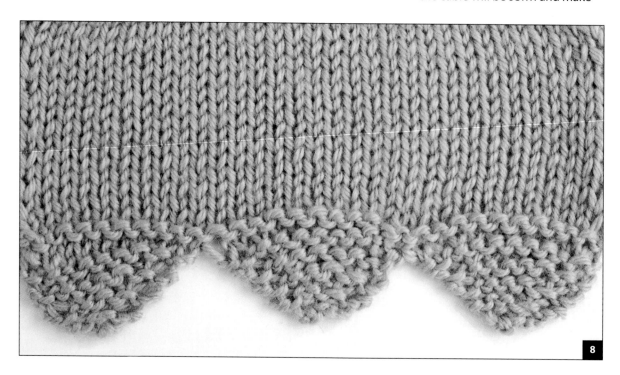

8

a cable band the same length. Photo 9 shows a centered 6-stitch cable with a purl stitch on either side of it; there is also a stockinette stitch selvage stitch on the edge that will to be used for seaming.

To make this cable band, use the same size needles as the body and cast on 9 stitches.

Rows 1 and 3 (RS): P1, k6, p1, k1 (selvage stitch).

Rows 2 and 4: P1, k1, p6, k1.

Row 5: P1, slip next 3 stitches to a cable needle and hold in back of work, k3, k3 from cable needle, p1, k1.

Row 6: Same as Row 2.

Repeat these 6 rows until the band is the same length as the edge you want to sew it to. Sew the band to the main fabric following Invisible Vertical to Horizontal seaming instructions on page 40.

Conversely, you can start by knitting a cable band that is as long as the desired width of your main fabric, and then pick up and knit stitches along the side of the cable band to begin the body. Remember to always include a selvage stitch into which to pick up your stitches.

I-cords

Adding a simple I-cord to the edge of any garment gives it a smooth, finished look. One easy way to make an I-cord border is to knit the I-cord separately from the garment, and then sew it to the main fabric using mattress stitch. Make your I-cord approximately as long as the edge that you will be sewing it to. Don't cut the yarn because you may find that you will need to make it longer (or shorter) to match the edge when sewing. When sewing horizontally, make sure to match the row gauge of the I-cord to the stitch gauge of the main fabric, skipping stitches on one side or another as necessary to keep the fabric from stretching or puckering. When sewing vertically, it's good to skip a stitch in the main fabric every once in a while so that the border is slightly shorter than the main fabric. Make sure to ease the corners for a flat edging. The example in Photo 10 shows the finished I-cord edge.

9

10

Horizontal applied I-cord/ I-cord bind-off

On last row, work I-cord bind-off across the top as follows:

Refer to Photo 11 and cast on 4 sts (provisionally if you're going to want to graft ends of I-cord together).

Slip the 4 sts to LH needle.

Row 1: K3, sl 1 st kwise, knit 1 st from main fabric, pass slipped st over (or ssk the 2 sts tog). DO NOT TURN. Pass the 4 I-cord sts back to RH needle.

Rep Row 1 until all sts on main fabric are bound-off.

Turn corner

Work 3 rows of unattached I-cord as follows: *K4, do not turn, pass I-cord sts back to RH needle; rep from * twice more.

Vertical applied I-cord

Row 1: K2, sl 1 st kwise, knit up 1 st from main fabric edge, pass slipped st over (or ssk the 2 sts tog). DO NOT TURN. Pass the 4 I-cord sts back to RH needle as shown in Photo 12. Rep Row 1 to next corner.

Photo 13 shows the completion of both methods.

Band & border variations

When working bands and borders, you can alter their height or width. Height can be adjusted by adding or eliminating rows; the width of a vertical band or border can be modified by increasing or decreasing the number of stitches cast on.

Color contrast

You can transform the entire look and feel of a finished piece by using a different yarn for the bands or borders—try using a different-colored yarn, or one with a different fiber composition or texture as shown in Photo 14.

If you choose to work a border in a contrasting color or yarn, make sure to knit on the right side or purl on the wrong side the last row before changing to the main color. This will ensure a clean line between colors.

13

14

Continuous

Another option is to continue part of the band pattern into the main body. Be sure to choose a pattern that will show up well against the main body stitch.

Photo 15 shows a 3-stitch cable that repeats along the border with one purl stitch between the cable repeats. Once the border height is reached, only two cables repeat (plus a purl stitch on either side of the cables) and are continued into the main body fabric, which here is stockinette stitch.

Ribbing

Ribbing can be both functional and decorative. Ribs give your edges strength and elasticity because they usually have a denser stitch gauge than the main fabric; they keep the edges from flaring out and help the piece hold its shape by bouncing back after being stretched.

There are many types of ribs. All ribbing is based on repeated knit and purl combinations. The most popular ribs are K1, P1 Rib or K2, P2 Rib, as shown in Photos 16 and 17. These ribs (also referred to as 1x1 or 2x2 ribs) are very elastic and easily bounce back to shape after being stretched. They make perfect neck edges.

15

16

Ribs do not have to have the same number of knit and purl stitches. Some pieces look best with K2, P1 Ribs or K1, P3 Ribs.
The combinations are endless.

Broken rib

In some cases, you may want the look of ribbing but not want the "pull-in" of a ribbed edge. Use a "broken" rib pattern instead—there are many! The Photo 18 example is produced by working a K1, P1 Rib on the right side and purling on the wrong side.

Two-color rib

Other inelastic ribbing options include multi-colored ribs. The two-color ribbing sample in Photo 19 is made by casting on with color A, after which all rows are worked Fair-Isle style, carrying the color not in use across the wrong side. Row 1 (right side) is worked by knitting 2 stitches in color A, then 2 stitches in color B and so on across the row. The rib is started on the second row (wrong side), with color A being purled and color B being knit. The rib continues on the following rows with the stitches and colors being worked as they present themselves.

Number of stitches to cast on for rib

Assuming that you will be seaming your garment using a mattress stitch and that you want your rib to be continuous around the bottom, make sure that you include a selvage stitch at each end of the row.

For a K1, P1 Rib, you should have an even number of stitches on the needle and your first right side row should be worked as follows: K1 (selvage st), *k1, p1; rep from * to last st, k1 (selvage stitch).

For a K2, P2 Rib, you should have a multiple of 4 stitches plus 2 and the first right side row should be worked as follows: K1 (selvage stitch), k1, *p2, k2; rep from * to end; the last k1 will be a selvage stitch. When you sew the back and front together, you will have a neat K2, P2 Rib all the way around. Adjust your stitch count for your main body fabric as necessary in the transition row between the ribbing and the body.

Final Thoughts

Any of these finishes can be used for just about any edge. Try a garter stitch band on the edge of a pocket or a seed stitch band on the edges of a garment's side vents. ■

19

Fully Fashioned Elements

By Jean Clement

Fully fashioned elements are techniques for creating knitted garments with the fashion sense man has been developing since he first began wearing animal skins.

In the beginning, man dressed himself with animal skins. Not very pretty, or very well fitting, but the skins did help protect man's body from the elements. As man grew and developed, so did his sense of fashion. Needles for sewing skins into shapes and pins to hold them together, lead to the eventual development of cloth—linen, silk and cotton. Cloth had so many more possibilities for creating garments, especially fashionable garments. Just look at the garments in Egyptian hieroglyphs. Move forward in time by a few thousand years, and knitting is beginning to appear in the Middle East. Now we have a type of cloth that is warm and malleable. We can be fashionable and warm.

The evolution of fashion just keeps getting better. Buttonholes make their first appearance in the 14th century. Just a short couple of hundred years later, shirts and trousers are common garments for men. And by the 17th century, silk stockings are a major industry in France.

So what does all this history have to do with fully fashioned elements in knitting? It shows us how man has come from dressing with animal skins to developing clothing that is not only practical but looks good and fits well.

In their most basic use, fully fashioned elements are the increases and decreases used to shape knitted garments. Specific placement of increases and decreases contour the knitted fabric for the desired shape. Fully fashioned elements are also used as design features—adding that fashion or couture-look. Did you know that when knitting instructions tell you to use a certain increase or decrease, it is because how that increase or decrease looks is part of the overall design features of that garment? Yes, there are times when the pattern instructions will leave it to the knitter to chose which increase or decrease to use. But if the increases and decreases are part of the design features, the pattern will specify which type to use.

As a shaping technique, fully fashioned elements are generally thought of most often as the decreases to shape an armhole, sleeve cap or neckline. Armhole shaping could be raglan, square, one shouldered or set-in. Necklines could be crewneck, V-neck, sweetheart, U-neck of varying depths or jewel neck. Fully fashioned increases are used to create all these shapes when the garment is worked from the top-down. The two elements

that distinguish "fully fashioned" shaping are that decreases and increases are directional (and mirrored) and are always worked at least one or two stitches in from the edge of the knitted fabric. This allows for a selvage edge that makes seaming of the garment easier and neater.

Shaping the armholes or neckline of a garment isn't the only use for fully fashioned elements, though. Fully fashioned decreases can outline the gores on a skirt worked from the hem to waist, and when working top-down, can create decorative vertical bustline darts. The same is true of fully fashioned increases for skirts worked from waist to hem or vertical bustline darts from the waist up.

While there are many types of increases and decreases, we are going to focus on just a few. The ones we will examine are the types that I see used most commonly. Most of these are worked essentially the same, whether you are working from the knit side or purl side of your work. The difference is that on the knit side, you work the increase or decrease using a knit stitch and on the purl side, you use a purl stitch. With that in mind, the swatches in the Photos show the fully fashioned elements worked on the knit side of the fabric.

Fully Fashioned Decreases

Perhaps the most common type of decrease is the knit two together—k2tog. This type of decrease produces a right-leaning stitch as shown in Photo 1.

To work a k2tog decrease, work to the stitch to be decreased, and then knit the first two stitches on the left needle together as one.

Worked on the purl side, this right-leaning decrease would be worked as p2tog.

When worked over several rows, with a plain row in between, this decrease shows a decorative line moving to the right.

The decrease that best mirrors the k2tog is slip, slip, knit—ssk. This decrease results in a left-leaning stitch, as in Photo 2.

Knitters, being the inventive people that they are, have come up with different ways to work the ssk decrease so that it looks best with their personal styles of knitting. One method is to slip the first stitch on the left needle knitwise to the right needle, repeat with the second stitch from the left needle; return both stitches to the left needle in the new orientation and knit them together through the back loops.

Worked from the purl side, both stitches are slipped knitwise as before, and then purled through the back loops.

The second method is to slip only the first stitch knitwise from the left to the right needle, return it to the left needle in the new orientation, and knit it together with the second stitch through the back loops. This will twist the second stitch, causing it to tuck under the first stitch more than the first method does. The finished appearance is very much the same

in both methods, although many knitters feel the second method produces a neater or straighter line when decreasing over several rows. This decrease results in a decorative line moving to the left.

Another common decrease is to pass a slipped stitch over a worked stitch. This type of decrease tends to look a bit flatter than decreases in which stitches are worked together.

For this decrease, refer to Photo 3, and work to the point at which a stitch will be decreased, slip one stitch knitwise to the right needle, knit the next stitch, and then pass the slipped stitch over the worked stitch and off the needle—skp.

This decrease leans left.

Worked from the purl side, the slipped stitch is slipped purlwise—spp (slip, purl, pass slipped stitch over). This is often used as the mirror decrease for skp.

When working a matching right-leaning decrease, it is possible to work a decrease from the knit side of your work that mirrors an skp. This keeps your decreases on the same row of your work where using the purl side spp decrease does not.

As in Photo 4, work to the point where your right leaning decrease will be—knit one stitch, slip the worked stitch to the left needle, pass the first unworked stitch on the left needle over the worked one, slip the worked stitch back to the right needle.

Photo 5 illustrates the last type of decrease we will discuss—the centered decrease. This decrease is generally used as a fully fashioned element when two stitches are to be decreased at once over several rows and a neat, straight, vertical line is desired.

Work to the number of stitches indicated in the pattern directions to the decrease point. Slip the next two stitches together as if to knit them together, knit the next stitch, and then pass the two stitches over the worked stitch—s2kp2.

To work this decrease from the purl side you must first slip the first two stitches separately knitwise to the right needle and return them to the left needle in the new orientation. Then slip both stitches together as if to purl through the back loops, purl the next stitch and pass the slipped stitches over.

All the decreases we have discussed here have variations in the total number of stitches that are to be decreased and whether the decreases are placed side by side or worked further apart. At times a designer may have you work a left leaning decrease near the left edge or a right leaning one on the right edge, depending on the look envisioned for a given design. In the Serene project included in the *Bonus Pattern Gallery*, fully fashioned decreases are used to shape the neckline and armholes. The neckline decreases are incorporated into the open work pattern while the armhole shaping is accomplished with the more visible left and right leaning decreases.

Fully Fashioned Increases

There are many common ways to work directional increases. As with fully fashioned decreases, the choice of increase to use depends on the overall design features; and the pattern designer will indicate if any particular increase should be used.

5

As shown in Photo 6, one of the first increases every beginning knitter learns is the bar increase. This increase leaves a "bar" of yarn across the front the increased stitch. It is very simple and decorative.

Work to the increase point—knit into the front of the next stitch, then knit into the back of the same stitch before dropping it from the left needle.

This increase will lean right or left when worked over several rows, depending on which stitch it is worked in. Increasing in the second stitch from a right edge results in a right leaning increase line. Working the increase in the third stitch from the left edge results in a left leaning increase. Both sides will appear to have two stitches between the selvage edge and the "bar" at the base of the increased stitch.

To work a bar increase from the purl side of the work, you would purl into the front of the stitch, and then purl into the back of the stitch before dropping the stitch from the left needle.

In the next group of photos, we have Make 1 Right and Make 1 Left. These increases use the strand that goes from one stitch to the next. They could also be worked over two rows using a yarn over.

To work a Make 1 Right, as in Photo 7, knit to the point where you will increase. Insert the tip of the left needle, from back to front, under the strand that connects the first stitches on each needle, and then knit into the front of the strand now on the left needle.

6

7

Knitting into the front of the strand will twist it, leaving only a tiny hole.

The mirror increase for Make 1 Right is Make 1 Left. It is also worked by picking up the connecting strand between the first stitches on each needle, as shown in the Photo 8 example.

Work to the point where you are going to increase, insert the tip of the right needle from back to front under the strand between the first stitches on each needle, place the strand on the left needle and twist it by knitting into the back of it.

As you look at these increases, you will see that the strand crosses in front to the right or left depending on whether it was picked up from the left and worked into the front or picked up from the right and worked into the back.

Working both the Make 1 Right and Make 1 Left increases from the purl side is the same as working them from the knit side. Pick up the connecting strand between the first stitches on each needle and purl into the back or front of it so that it is twisted.

The alternative method of "making one" is to make a yarn over at the increase point and on the following row work into it, twisting it to close the larger hole a yarn over generally leaves. There will still be a tiny hole the same as when the increase is made into the connecting strand.

One of my favorite increases is the Lifted Increase. It is easily worked as single increases on opposite sides of the knitted piece, or on both sides of a central stitch resulting in a neat, vertical increase line. No matter where this increase is used, it looks good and does not leave any holes.

To work a right-leaning lifted increases, work to where the increase will be. As shown in Photo 9, insert the right needle tip from back to front into the right side of the stitch below the first stitch on the left needle, placing the lifted stitch on the left needle, Knit the stitch above as you usually would.

Working this increase every other row creates a line that moves to the right.

On the purl side of the fabric, work to the increase point, insert the left needle tip from front to back into the side of the stitch two rows below the stitch on the right needle, and purl into the front of it.

The left-leaning Lifted Increase matches the right-leaning Lifted Increase exactly as presented in Photo 10.

This increase is worked by inserting the left needle tip from back to front into the right side of the stitch two rows below the first stitch on the right needle, lifting the stitch onto the left needle, and then knitting into the back of this stitch.

When worked over several rows, this increase creates a line that moves to the left.

To work a left-leaning increase on the purl side of the fabric, with the right needle tip pick up from back to front the right side of the stitch directly below the first stitch on the left needle and purl into the front of it. It will seem as if the lifted stitch is twisted when you put it on the left needle, but it is not.

Now just imagine the fashion statement that early man would have made if he had only known how to knit and add fully fashioned elements to his garments. With your newly found skills, you can create garments that both fit well and make a fashion statement. ∎

10

The Art of Short Rows

By Jean Clement

The use of short rows are indispensable when it comes to shaping your garments in a multitude of imaginative ways.

Do you look at a pattern incorporating short rows and cringe? Do you wish your short rows looked better or less visible? Are you a new knitter wondering what short rows are? If you answered yes to any of these questions, then read on and join me on this little journey into short rows—when to use them and how to make them.

Short rows are one of the techniques every knitter should have in her "knitting toolbox." The simple act of working part way across a row, and then turning and working back without completing the remainder of the row has many uses.

Uses for Short Rows

The most familiar use of short rows is for bust shaping—short rows create extra fabric that allows the garment to fit smoothly over the bustline. But that's not the only use for short rows.

Sock knitters use short rows to turn the heel of a sock. Have you ever known anyone who has developed a dowager's hump or has a portly tummy? What about someone with a high hip? Short rows can be used to make alterations to a garment, adding extra fabric where needed so the hemline is even and the garment fits well over the wearer's unique body parts. Short rows can also be used to create an A-line skirt or body of a top worked side to side. A shawl collar lies so much better when constructed with short rows. And using short rows to slope the shoulders of a garment results in a more flattering and proper fit, and can be seamed more easily than stair-step, bound-off shoulders. Expectant mothers can use short rows to turn a garment into maternity wear. Short rows can even be used to create interesting color patterns for an afghan, pillow or sweater. The uses for short rows are limited only by the knitter's imagination.

There are many ways of working short rows, and being the creative people that knitters are, different methods are being developed all the time. In this article, we are going to focus on two methods of working short rows: The first, known as "Wrap & Turn," is the most well-known method; the second, "Japanese Short Rows," is a lesser known, but excellent method. Both methods are easy to learn and master, so let's get started.

Wrap & Turn Short Rows

A short row is created by working partway across a row, and then turning and working the next row without having worked all the stitches in the first row. Most of the time we want to hide our turning point so the short rows are not readily visible and no holes are created. This is where the "wrap" comes in. The stitch at the turning point is wrapped and when we are ready to work a full row, the wrap will be picked up and worked with the wrapped stitch.

Let's take it step by step

Using worsted weight yarn, knit a swatch in stockinette stitch about 20 stitches wide and two inches long. We'll work our first short row from the front or knit side. Knit the first 10 stitches, then bring the yarn between the needles to the front of the work. Now slip the next stitch purlwise to the right-hand needle, and then move the yarn between the needles to the back of the work. This maneuver is what wraps the stitch as shown in Photo 1.

The next step is to turn the work, return the first stitch (the stitch you slipped previously) back to the now right-hand needle—do not work it—then purl the rest of the stitches. When you turn your work to purl back, be sure to not pull the wrap too tightly or leave it too loose; you want to match your tension as much as possible. With the front (knit side) of your swatch facing you, you will see that the first 10 stitches have been worked two rows more than the last 10 stitches and stitch 11 has a "wrap" of yarn around its base. You've just worked one set of short rows.

Now we're going to work a full row across our swatch, hiding the wrap so the short row is less visible. Knit the first 10 stitches of your swatch. Slip the next stitch onto your right needle, and then insert your left needle tip under the wrap, lifting the wrap onto the left needle as shown in Photo 2, and then return the slipped stitch back on the left needle.

Now knit the wrap together with the stitch it was wrapping, just like a k2tog decrease, and continue knitting to the end of the row. With practice, you will be able to use your right needle to pick up the wrap and knit it together with the wrapped stitch without slipping the wrapped stitch first to the right needle, and then back again.

The procedure to work a "wrap & turn" short row from the purl side of your work is nearly the same as working it from the knit side. Work a few more rows in your swatch, then work a purl row to your turning point, move the yarn to the knit side of the work, slip the next stitch purlwise, and bring the yarn to the purl side of the work, as in Photo 3.

Turn your work, return the slipped stitch to the needle now in your right hand and complete the short row. As you come to the wrapped stitch on the next full row, you will work the wrap and wrapped stitch together just as you did before. Purl the first 10 stitches, then from the knit side—which is the side facing away from you, insert your right-hand needle under the wrap, lift it to your left needle and purl it together with the stitch it wrapped. Picking up the wrap from the knit side is the easiest and neatest way to work a purl side wrap with its wrapped stitch, as shown in Photo 4.

There are times when you can work "wrap & turn" short rows and not hide the wraps. One is when working in garter stitch. Because the wrap matches the garter stitch very closely, it is not usually necessary, or preferable, to hide the wraps. Another is when you want the decorative effect created in stockinette stitch by not hiding the wraps; the wrapped stitches will have a bar across the front of them. You can also create an eyelet effect, which will also result from not picking up the wraps.

Photo 5 shows a swatch with wrap & turn short rows worked for bustline shaping, which you can put to use in the "Serene" pattern included in the final chapter of this book.

Japanese Short Rows

The second way of working short rows is known as "Japanese Short Rows" or the "catch" method. I prefer this method because I think it produces a very tidy, as-invisible-as-you-can-get turning point with no holes. This method is no more difficult to work than wrap & turn, but it does require paying a little more attention.

The first thing you need to know is that when using this method, the short rows are turned the same, whether you are turning from the knit side or purl side of your work. However, the gap will be closed differently depending on which side you are working from.

We'll start by knitting a stockinette stitch swatch about 20 stitches wide and two inches long just as we did for the wrap & turn method. For the first part of the short row, knit 10 stitches. Turn your work, right there in the middle of the row—no wrapping. As Photo 6 illustrates, a split-ring marker can be placed around the working yarn at this point before completing the purl side of the short row.

Slip the first stitch purlwise and purl the remaining nine stitches. Keep the slipped stitch the same gauge as the rest of your work—do not pull it too tightly or leave it loose. As before, you will have 10 stitches that have been worked two rows more than the remaining 10 stitches.

Now we're going to work a full row, joining our short rows to the rest of the swatch, working from the knit side. Knit across the first 10 stitches, including the slipped stitch. At this point, look at the back of your work. You will be picking up the strand of yarn that connects the slipped stitch (now in the second row below your needle) with the stitch immediately to the left as in Photo 7.

Looking at your work from the right side, this would be the strand of yarn that connects the slipped stitch with its neighboring stitch on the right. Since we placed a split-ring marker around our working yarn in the first step, this strand is easy to see.

Insert the tip of your left needle into this strand from the top down, lift it onto the needle, and then knit it together with the next stitch. Pull up on the pin/marker and place the resulting loop on the left needle as shown in Photo 8, then knit it together with the next stitch.

In Japanese short rows, the procedure to join the short row from the purl side of your work to the rest of your knitting is a little different. Since we are picking up a strand from the back—or purl side—of the work, we need make sure that strand ends up behind the stitch it will be purled together with.

7

8

Work a few more rows on your swatch, then on a purl row work the first 10 stitches, place a marker as we did before, turn your work as shown in Photo 9, slip the first stitch purlwise, keeping your tension even with the rest of your work and knit to the end of the short row.

This next step is really much simpler than it may seem at first. Purl the first 10 stitches, including the slipped stitch—you are now at your turning point. Just as we did for the knit side, you want to identify the strand that connects the slipped stitch with its neighboring stitch to the right as illustrated in Photo 10.

Slip the next stitch from the left needle to the right needle, then insert your left needle into the connecting strand you have already identified, from the bottom up and onto the left needle.

Having placed a split-ring marker around the working yarn in the turning step, pull up on the pin or marker and place the resulting loop on the left needle as in Photo 11.

Return the first stitch back to the left needle, and then purl that stitch together with the lifted loop. Finish working your row. That's all there is to it!

For Photo 12, the swatch shows bust shaping using Japanese short rows. Compare this with the wrap & turn short rows in Photo 5 and chose the method you like more.

Now that you know how to work short rows, you can fine-tune the fit of your garments—making alterations as needed and adding fabric to improve the fit of a bust line—or knit a fabulous afghan using color changes created with short rows.

Once you have practiced with your swatches a bit and are comfortable with either short-row technique, turn to the *Bonus Project Gallery* and use your new skills to knit "Serene," on page 148, a top designed just for you! ∎

Enticing Embellishments

By Myra Wood

Just a touch of ruffle or an added detail of embroidery can transform an ordinary knitted item into a truly unique and special project.

Crocheted Edgings

One of the handiest tools in a knitter's bag is the trusty crochet hook. The combination of knitwear and crocheted edgings creates a beautifully finished and decorative effect.

Just a few simple crochet stitches can make a big difference on a hem or sleeve edge.

Crochet Picot Bind-Off

Step 1: Finish the last row of knitting, ending on the wrong side; do not bind off. With the right side facing you, insert crochet hook (same size as needles used to make main garment) into the first two stitches as if to knit, yarn over, pull loop through, sliding stitches off the left needle.

Step 2: 2 single crochet stitches: *Insert the hook knitwise into the next live stitch, yarn over, pull a loop through, yarn over, pull through both stitches on the hook to complete single crochet. Repeat from * once more.

Step 3: Make picot: Chain 3, slip stitch into the last single crochet to complete the picot.

Step 4: *Single crochet in next 3 stitches; make picot; repeat from * across. Photo 1 is the completion on Steps 1–4.

The picot bind-off can also be worked over a bound-off edge by inserting the hook into the edge of the finished item and single crocheting along the edge, adding picots as desired, as shown in Photo 2.

Shell Stitch Edging

Step 1: With the right side of the finished fabric facing you, insert crochet hook (same size as the needles used to make main garment) under both legs of the end stitch or row where the edge is to begin. Yarn over with new yarn, pull loop through, chain 1, as shown in Photo 3.

Step 2: Skip the next 2 stitches, work 5 double crochets in next stitch, skip 2 stitches, single crochet in next stitch, as shown in Photo 4.

Step 3: Repeat Step 2 as needed evenly around edge as shown in Photo 5.

Crab Stitch
(reverse single crochet)

Step 1: With the right side of the fabric facing you and working from left to right (if right-handed work from right to left if left-handed), insert crochet hook (same size as needles used to make main garment) under both legs of the end stitch, or row where the edge is to begin, yarn over, pull through, chain 1.

Step 2: Insert hook from front to back in next stitch to the right (or left if left-handed). Yarn over and pull through, twisting the hook so that the stitch twists.

Step 3: Yarn over and pull through both loops on the hook, as shown in Photo 6.

Continue to work from left to right (or right to left if left-handed), twisting the crochet hook as you insert it into the next stitch. The finished top edge will have the appearance of a twisted cord as shown in Photo 7.

I-Cord

Single I-Cord

Cast 4 stitches onto a double-point needle.

Step 1: Knit across, as shown in Photo 8.

Step 2: Without turning, slide the 4 stitches to the right end of the same needle, as shown in Photo 9.

Step 3: Bring the yarn from the last stitch knit across the back of the work and knit from right to left across the row.

As in Photo 10, repeat Steps 2 and 3 until the cord is the desired length.

The I-cord can be sewn to a finished edge or can be applied as a surface embellishment. Tie it into a bow for a lovely accent, as shown in Photo 11.

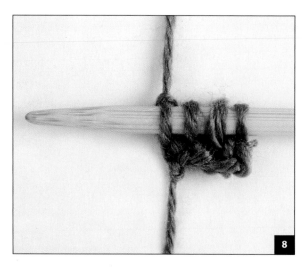

Ruffles

Add a ruffled edge to the last row, or a finished edge, by picking up all the stitches along the edge.

Step 1: As demonstrated in Photo 12, knit into the front and back of each stitch to double the number of stitches on the needle (kfb).

Step 2: Purl across.

Step 3: Knit across.

Step 4: To keep an elastic edge, single crochet bind off all the stitches as follows: Insert crochet hook into first stitch, yarn over and pull a loop through. Insert hook into next stitch, yarn over and pull through a loop. There are now 2 loops on the hook. Yarn over and pull through both loops. Continue to single crochet the stitches off the needle.

The size and amount of ruffling can easily be modified by adding more rows, as you can see in Photos 13 and 14. Experiment with adding another row of increases to exaggerate the curves.

Embroidery

Embroidery accents add a special touch to any knitted item. Embroidery stitches can be used with various yarns in either symmetrical or random patterns. Because knitted stitches are looser than woven fabric, it's best to use an appropriate weight of contrasting yarn to show off the embroidery to its fullest. Use a blunt tapestry needle with a big eye for stitching. In all cases, avoid making knots on the back of the work; weave in the tail rather than creating a knot to start your work.

Single Chain Stitch

Step 1: Bring the threaded needle from the back of the work to the front. Slide the needle back through the same hole and out through the front of the fabric about an ⅛ inch away, catching a loop under the needle.

Step 2: Pull the needle through without tightening the loop. The working yarn will be on the inside of the loop.

Step 3: Insert the needle from front to back just on the outside of the yarn to anchor the loop, as presented in Photo 15.

Running Chain Stitch

Step 1: Bring the threaded needle to the front of the work. In one move, slide the needle back through the same hole and out through the front of the fabric about ⅛ inch away, catching a loop under the needle.

Step 2: Pull the needle through without tightening the loop. The working yarn will be on the inside of the loop.

Referring to Photo 16, repeat Steps 1 and 2 to desired length of chain.

15

16

Feather Stitch

Step 1: Bring the threaded needle to the front of the work at the top of where the feather chain will begin.

Step 2: In one move, slide the needle through the knitting ⅛ inch to the right and bring it back out ⅛ inch below, directly between the 2 points, catching the working yarn under the needle.

Step 3: Pull the needle through without tightening too much.

Refer to Photo 17, and continue Step 2 and 3 either to the right or to the left as desired.

Beaded Embroidery

Step 1: After creating a running chain, straight stitch 2 lines at the bottom of each chain through the same hole, as shown in Photo 18.

Step 2: Sew beads at the ends of the lines with upholstery thread that matches the main fabric to accent as desired, as shown in Photo 19.

Blanket Stitch

The blanket stitch is a wonderful finish to cuff, collar and hem edges.

Step 1: Working left to right at the edge of your piece, bring the threaded needle to the front of the work.

Step 2: In one move, insert the needle ¼ inch above and ⅛ inch to the right and back out even with the original point, catching the working yarn under the needle, as shown in Photo 20.

Step 3: Pull the needle through, tightening the right angle created.

Referring to Photos 20 and 21, repeat Steps 2 and 3 evenly across the edge. Photo 22 shows the completed Blanket Stitch edge. The length and width between stitches can vary as desired.

French Knot

Step 1: Bring the threaded needle to the front of the work.

Step 2: With the point of the needle facing down, wind the yarn around the needle clockwise two times.

Step 3: Bring the working yarn under the needle, catching the yarn to lock the stitch in place. Slide the knot to the fabric and insert the needle back into the fabric on the other side of the same stitch where you began.

Step 4: Holding the knot on the front of the fabric, take the needle through the knot and pull excess yarn to the back of the fabric as shown in Photo 23.

Straight Stitch/Satin Stitch

Step 1: Bring the threaded needle to the front of the work.

Step 2: In one move, insert needle ⅛–¼ inch away.

For the satin stitch, continue to do straight stitches next to each other to fill in a desired shape as shown in Photo 24.

Combining Embroidery Stitches

Any of these stitches can be combined in a freestyle method to create gorgeous floral accents, as illustrated in Photo 25. Start with the branches and leaves and build the flowers over them.

Duplicate Stitch

The duplicate stitch is an embroidery stitch that mimics the actual knitted stitches of a finished piece to add color and pattern to the surface.

Avoid knots on the wrong side of your work by weaving in the tail.

Step 1: Bring the threaded needle to the front of the work at the bottom V of a knit stitch.

Step 2: Follow the path of that stitch by inserting the needle through the 2 legs of the stitch above.

Step 3: Insert the needle back through the original point.

Continue to repeat Steps 1 and 2, while referring to Photos 26 and 27, in any direction you like, always following the path of the knitted stitches.

26

27

Appliqué & 3 Dimensional Elements

Individual elements can be knitted and added to the surface to add 3-D interest. Sew them flat or let them hang freely.

Ruffly Rose

Small (large) Instructions are given for smaller size, with larger size in parentheses. When only 1 number is given, it applies to both sizes.

While referring to Photo 28, cast on 6 (10) sts.

Row 1 and all WS rows: Knit.

Row 2: *K1, M1; rep from * to last st, k1.

Row 4: K1, *yo, k1; rep from * to end.

Row 6: K1, *M1, k1; rep from * to end.

Row 8: Crochet bind-off: Insert hook kwise, yo, pull loop through, yo, pull through both stitches on hook to complete single crochet, ch 1 to last st, pull yarn through.

Twist flower into desired shape and stitch in place at base as shown in Photo 29.

Leaves

Cast on 5.

Row 1 and all WS rows: Purl across.

Row 2: K1, kfb, k1, kfb, k1—7 sts.

Row 4: K2, kfb, k1, kfb, k2—9 sts.

Row 6: Knit.

Rows 8, 10 and 12: K1, ssk, knit to last 3 sts, k2tog, k1—3 sts.

Row 14: S1, k1, psso.

Larger or smaller leaves can be made in the same manner by working more or fewer increase rows, and then decreasing down to 3 stitches for the tip, as shown in Photo 30.

28

29

30

Single Bobble

Step 1: Create a knitted diamond as follows.

Row 1: Cast on 1 st, knit in front, back, front of same st to make 3 sts.

Row 2 and all WS rows: Purl across.

Row 3: Kfb, k1, kfb—5 sts.

Row 5: Sl 1, k1, psso, k1, k2tog.

Row 7: K3tog. Cut yarn and pull tail through, as shown in Photo 31.

Step 2: Tie tails together tightly on wrong side as shown in Photo 32.

Step 3: Thread a yarn needle with each tail and bring through opposite open sides to create a ball. Tie together tightly as in Photo 33.

Step 4: With the existing tails remaining, as shown in Photo 34, sew finished bobble to surface of fabric.

Fringe and Tassels

Single Knotted Fringe

Step 1: Cut equal lengths of yarn twice the length of the desired finished fringe.

Step 2: Insert a crochet hook from front to back into the last row or edge of finished work. Fold cut yarn in half and pull center of fold through to front.

Step 3: Take both ends and bring them through the loop; pull tightly, referring to Photo 35.

Repeat across the entire edge evenly to complete the fringe as shown in Photo 36.

Trim to even.

Single Tassel

Step 1: Wrap yarn around a piece of cardboard the length of desired finished tassel.

Step 2: Thread a yarn needle with 12 inches of the same yarn and thread behind the loops on one side near the top. Tie that yarn tightly around the loops on the top edge. Cut across the bottom edge to make a bunch of strands that is gathered in the center as in Photo 37.

Step 3: Make a slip knot and slide it over the top of the folded tassel. Tie tightly and continue to wind around the tassel as desired. Cut the yarn and thread it back onto the needle. Insert the needle through the wraps and pull tightly out through the bottom. Cut to the length of other tassel fringes.

Step 3: Use the top tails to tie and secure to fabric, as shown in Photo 38, and the completed edge in Photo 39.

Looped Fringe

Step 1: With the wrong side of the fabric facing you and working right to left with a crochet hook, attach yarn from wrong side at the edge or last row with a slip stitch, chain 1 to secure.

Step 2: Insert the hook into the next stitch and bring the yarn over a piece of cardboard the height of the desired fringe. Pull a loop through two loops on hook.

Step 3: Yarn over and pull through both loops on the hook.

Step 4: Insert the hook into the same stitch and bring the yarn over the cardboard again. Pull a loop through two loops on hook.

Step 5: Yarn over and pull through both loops on hook.

Refer to Photo 40, and continue Steps 2–5 evenly across the edge, working into each stitch. See Photo 41 for completed edge. ■

40

41

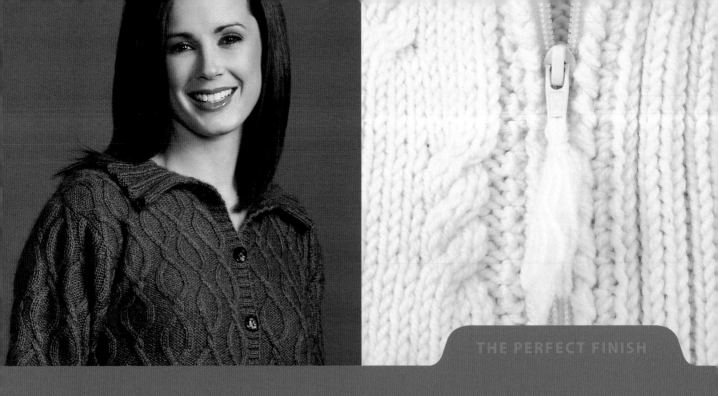

Bonus Project Gallery

This is where our designers put it all together and share some fabulous projects, showcasing many of the finishing techniques found throughout the book. If you're in the mood for a hoodie with cabled accents, then you'll love Amy Polcyn's Casual Cabled Hoodie. If you're ready for a challenge, then go for it with Leslye Solomon's Double-Zip Cardigan.

Wild Flower Purse

Design by Myra Wood

Show off your embellishment skills and transform a plain purse into a one-of-a-kind work of wearable art.

Materials

Mission Falls 136 Merino Superwash (DK weight; 100% superwash merino wool; 136 yds/50g per ball): 1 ball each cocoa #007 (MC) and amethyst #023 (B); 50 yds each aster #0536 (C), pistachio #028 (D), mallow #025(E), russet #010 (F), curry #013 (G) and raspberry #029 (H)

Size 5 (3.75mm) straight and double-point needles or size needed to obtain gauge

Size F/5 (3.5mm) crochet hook

Blunt tapestry needle

3½-inch-square cardboard for tassels

Skill Level

 INTERMEDIATE

Finished Size

8½ inches wide x 8 inches high (not including strap)

Gauge

24 sts and 32 rows = 4 inches/10cm in St st.

To save time, take time to check gauge.

Special Techniques

Provisional cast-on: see page26.

Crochet picot bind-off, embroidery, bobbles and I-cord, see Enticing Embellishments chapter (page 113).

Bag

With MC, use a provisional method to cast on 45 sts.

Work in St st until piece measures 6¼ inches and mark both sides of fabric to indicate bottom.

Continue in St st for another 6¼ inches.

Place live sts on waste yarn.

Remove provisional cast-on and place live stitches on waste yarn.

Block rectangle to 8½ inches wide by 12½ inches long, making sure to square corners at right angles.

Fold rectangle in half at marked positions.

Sew side seams using mattress stitch.

Eyelets and top edge

Slip 90 live sts to 3 dpns distributed 28-35-28.

Join MC at side edge and knit 7 rnds.

Eyelet rnd: K5, yo, *k2tog, k7, yo; rep from * around to last 4 sts, k2tog, k2.

Knit 7 rnds.

Change to B. Knit 3 rnds.

With crochet hook, work picot bind-off as follows: *6 sc, picot; rep from * around, slip stitch to join, cut yarn and weave in end.

Embellishments

Following charts, duplicate stitch pat across upper and lower edge of front and back 1 inch from top and bottom.

With D, embroider stems with running chain and feather stitches.

With D, knit 3 leaves and sew with whipstitch to surface of bag.

With E, make 4 bobbles and sew to surface of bag for flower centers; with H, embroider petals around bobbles using single chain stitches.

With F, embroider 3 flower centers using satin stitch; with G, surround each center with petals using single chain stitches.

STITCH AND COLOR KEY
- ◼ Cocoa (MC) - Main fabric
- ◻ Duplicate stitch with mallow (E)
- ◼ Duplicate stitch with raspberry (H)
- ◻ Duplicate stitch with pistachio (D)

DUPLICATE STITCH CHARTS

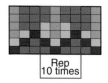

Rep 10 times

TOP CHART

DUPLICATE STITCH CHARTS

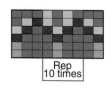

Rep 10 times

BOTTOM CHART

STITCH AND COLOR KEY

▥	Satin stitch with F
✑	Knitted bobble with E
●	French knot with C
◊	Single chain stitch with G & H
⌇	Running chain stitch with D
⋎	Feather stitch with D
◗	Knitted leaf with D

Leaves and bobbles are knitted separately and appliqéd on.

With C, embroider French knot accents as desired.

Drawstring

With B, cast on 4 sts, leaving a 6-inch tail.

Work I-cord 32 inches long.

Weave in ends.

Weave I-cord through eyelets starting at center hole on front of bag.

Strap

With B, cast on 4 sts, leaving a 15-inch tail.

Work I-cord 52 inches long.

Bind off, leaving a 15-inch tail.

Matching ends of I-cord to each side of bag, pin in position from bottom to top.

Using tails and mattress stitch, sew I-cord to sides from bottom edge to 1 inch below top edge on each side.

Tassels

Make 2 tassels by winding yarn around 3½-inch cardboard 50 times.

Sew each tassel to bottom corners. ∎

Cable Swing Sweater

Design by Arenda Holladay

Try your finishing skills with the classic A-line swing sweater with meandering cablework.

Materials

Rowan Kid Classic (worsted weight; 70% lambswool/26% kid mohair/4% nylon; 153 yds/50g per ball): 11 (12, 13, 14) skeins bear #817

Size 4 (3.5mm) needles

Size 5 (3.75mm) needles or size needed to obtain gauge

Cable needle

6 ½ inch buttons

Skill Level

 INTERMEDIATE

Sizes

Woman's small (medium, large/extra-large, 2X-large) Instructions are given for smallest size, with larger sizes in parentheses. When only 1 number is given, it applies to all sizes.

Finished Measurements

Chest: 36 (42, 48, 52) inches

Length to shoulders: 24 (25½, 27, 28½) inches

Gauge

26 sts and 32 rows = 4 inches/10cm in Cable pat st with larger needles.

To save time, take time to check gauge.

Special Abbreviations

Lifted Increase Left (L1-L): Working in pat, k1 (or p1) in st 2 rows below last st worked.

Lifted Increase Right (L1-R): Working in pat, k1 (or p1) in st in row below next st.

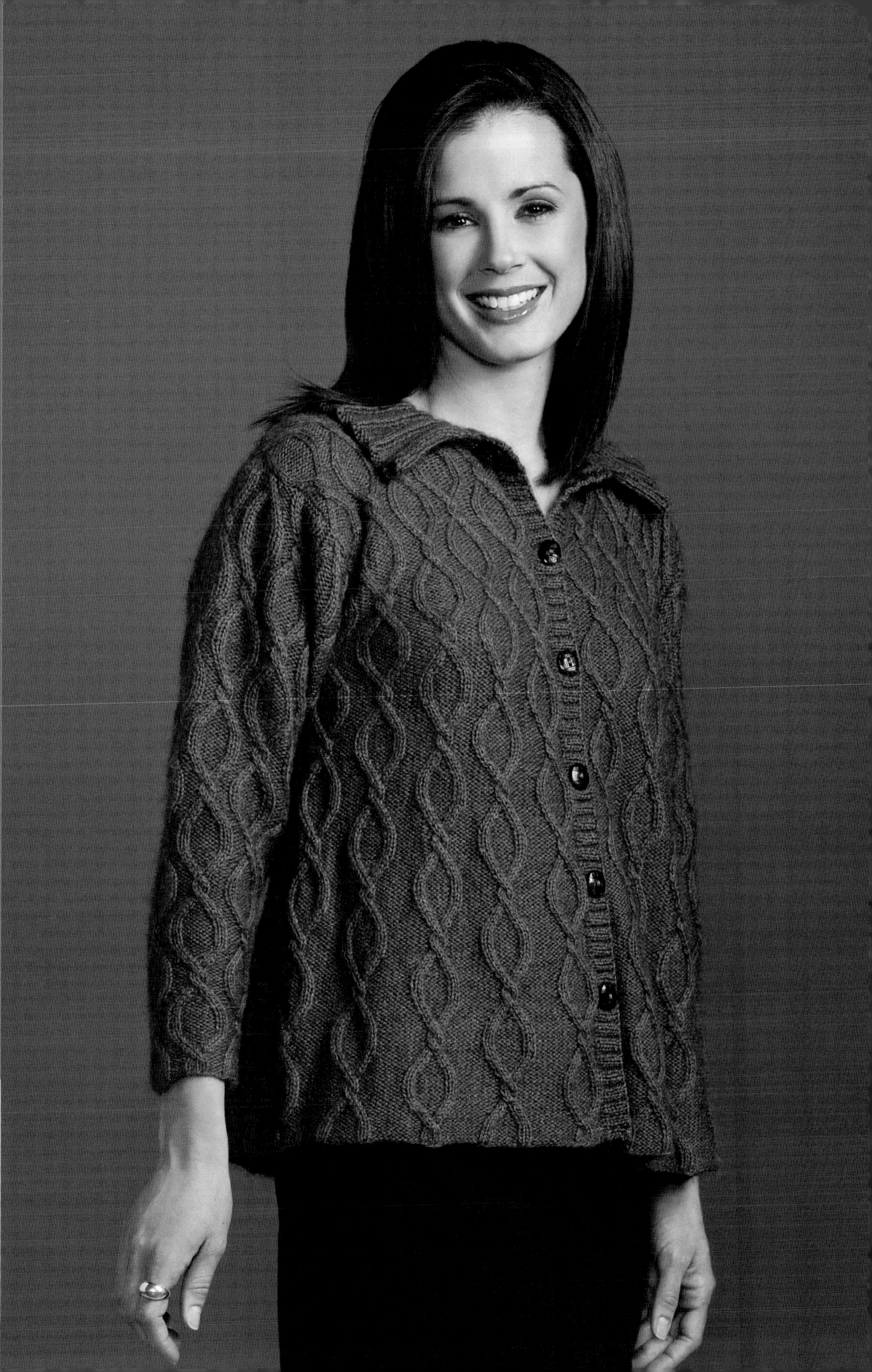

Pattern Stitches

Cable A (10-st panel)

Cable B (10-st panel)

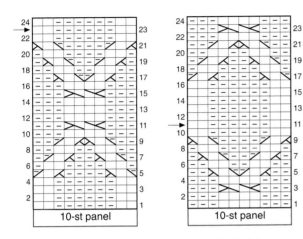

CABLE A   CABLE B

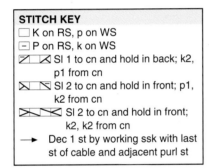

STITCH KEY

☐ K on RS, p on WS

⊟ P on RS, k on WS

SI 1 to cn and hold in back; k2, p1 from cn

SI 2 to cn and hold in front; p1, k2 from cn

SI 2 to cn and hold in front; k2, k2 from cn

→ Dec 1 st by working ssk with last st of cable and adjacent purl st

Pattern Note

Ssk decreases are used to shape the sweater and are made by working the last knit stitch in the cable on Row 23 of Cable A and Row 11 of Cable B and the purl stitch next to it. The result is an almost invisible decrease.

Back

With larger needles, cast on 162 (194, 226, 258) sts.

Row 1 (RS): K1 (selvage st), *work Row 1 of Cable A, p6, work Row 1 of Cable B, p6; rep from * to last st, k1 (selvage st).

Row 2 (WS): P1, *k6, work Row 2 of Cable B, k6, work Row 2 of Cable A; rep from * to last st, p1.

Rep Rows 1 and 2.

Beg with Row 3 of charts, work even, maintaining 6 sts between the cable pats, ending on Row 22 of charts.

Dec row 1 (RS): K1, *work to last st in Cable A, ssk, p5, work Cable B, p6; rep from * to last st, k1—157 (188, 219, 250) sts.

Work even, ending on Row 10 of charts.

Dec row 2: K1, *work Cable A, p5, work to last st in Cable B, ssk, p5; rep from * to last st, k1—152 (182, 212, 242) sts.

Work even, ending on Row 22 of charts.

Dec row 3: K1, *work to last st in Cable A, ssk, p4, work Cable B, p5; rep from * to last st, k1—147 (176, 205, 234) sts.

Work even, ending on Row 10 of charts.

Dec row 4: K1, *work Cable A, p4, work to last st in Cable B, ssk, p4; rep from * to last st, k1—142 (170, 198, 226) sts.

Work even, ending on Row 22 of charts.

Dec row 5: K1, *work to last st in Cable A, ssk, p3, work Cable B, p4; rep from * to last st, k1—137 (164, 191, 218) sts.

Work even, ending on Row 10 of charts.

Dec row 6: K1, *work Cable A, p3, work to last st in Cable B, ssk, p3; rep from * to last st, k1—132 (158, 184, 210) sts.

Work even, ending on Row 22 of charts.

Dec row 7: K1, *work to last st in Cable A, ssk, p2, work Cable B, p3; rep from * to last st, k1—127 (152, 177, 202) sts.

Work even, ending on Row 10 of charts.

Dec row 8: K1, *work Cable A, p2, work to last st in Cable B, ssk, p2; rep from * to last st, k1—122 (146, 170, 194) sts.

Work even, ending on Row 22 of charts.

Dec row 9: K1, *work to last st in Cable A, ssk, p1, work Cable B, p2; rep from * to last st, k1—117 (140, 163, 186) sts.

Work even, ending on Row 10 of charts.

Dec row 10: K1, *work Cable A, p1, work to last st in Cable B, ssk, p1; rep from * to last st, k1—112 (134, 156, 178) sts.

Work even, ending on Row 20 of charts.

Dec row 11: K1, *work to last st in Cable Chart A, ssk, work Cable B, p1; rep from * to last st, k1—107 (128, 149, 170) sts.

Work even, ending on Row 10 of charts.

Dec row 12: K1, *work Cable A, work to last st in Cable B, ssk; rep from * to last st, k1—102 (122, 142, 162) sts.

Work even until piece measures approx 24 (25½, 27, 28½) inches, ending on Row 12 or 24 of charts.

Bind off.

Left Front

With larger needles, cast on 82 (98, 114, 130) sts.

Row 1 (RS): K1, *work Row 1 of Cable A, p6, work Row 1 of Cable B, p6; rep from * until 17 (1, 17, 1) st(s) rem, work Row 1 of Cable A 1 (0, 1, 0) time(s), p6 (0, 6, 0), k1.

Row 2 (WS): P1, k6, work Row 2 of Cable A 1 (0, 1, 0) time(s), *k6, work Row 2 of Cable B, k6, work Row 2 of Cable A; rep from * to last st, p1.

Rep Rows 1 and 2.

Beg with Row 3 of charts, work even, maintaining 6 sts between the cable pats, ending on Chart Row 22.

Work the Dec rows as for the back, making the decs for Cable A on Row 23 and decs for Cable B on Row 11. The number of sts remaining after each Dec row is as follows:

Dec row 1: 79 (95, 110, 126) sts.

Dec row 2: 77 (92, 107, 122) sts.

Dec row 3: 74 (89, 103, 118) sts.

Dec row 4: 72 (86, 100, 114) sts.

Dec row 5: 69 (83, 96, 110) sts.

Dec row 6: 67 (80, 93, 106) sts.

Dec row 7: 64 (77, 89, 102) sts.

Dec row 8: 62 (74, 86, 98) sts.

Dec row 9: 59 (71, 82, 94) sts.

Dec row 10: 57 (68, 79, 90) sts.

Dec row 11: 54 (65, 75, 86) sts.

Dec row 12: 52 (62, 72, 82) sts.

Work even until piece measures 22 (23½, 25, 26½) inches, ending with a WS row.

Shape front neck

Bind off 10 (10, 15, 15) sts at neck edge once and 5 sts every RS row 2 (2, 3, 3) times—32 (42, 42, 52) sts.

Work even until piece measures 24 (25½, 27, 28½) inches.

Bind off.

Right Front

With larger needles, cast on 82 (98, 114, 130) sts.

Row 1 (RS): K1, work Row 1 of Cable B 1 (0, 1, 0) time(s), p6 (0, 6, 0), *work Row 1 of Cable A, p6, work Row 1 of Cable B, p6; rep from * to last st, k1.

Row 2 (WS): P1, *k6, work Row 2 of Cable B, k6, work Row 2 of Cable A; rep from * to last 17 (1, 17, 1) sts, p6 (0, 6, 0), work Row 2 of Cable B 1 (0, 1, 0) time(s), p1.

Rep Rows 1 and 2.

Continue as for left front, working the Dec rows as for back.

The number of sts rem after each Dec row is the same as for the left front.

Work even until piece measures 22 (23½, 25, 26½) inches, ending with a RS row.

Shape front neck

Bind off at neck edge 10 (10, 15, 15) sts once, then 5 sts [every WS row] 2 (2, 3, 3) times—32 (42, 42, 52) sts.

Work even until piece measures 24 (25½, 27, 28½) inches, ending on Chart Row 12 or 24.

Bind off.

Sleeves

With larger needles, cast on 52 (56, 62, 66) sts.

Row 1 (RS): K1, p0 (2, 0, 2), *work Row 1 of Cable A, work Row 1 of Cable B; rep from * to last 1 (3, 11, 13) st(s), work Row 1 of Cable B 0 (0, 1, 1) time(s), p0 (2, 0, 2), k1.

Row 2 (WS): P1, k0 (2, 0, 2), work Row 1 of Cable A 0 (1, 0, 1) time(s), *work Row 1 of Cable B, work Cable A; rep from * to last 1 (3, 1, 3) st(s), k0 (2, 0, 2), p1.

Rep Rows 1 and 2.

Beg with Row 3 of charts, work 2 rows even.

Inc row (RS): Work 2 sts, L1-L, work to last 2 sts, L1-R, work 2 sts—54 (58, 64, 68) sts.

Continue in pat and rep Inc row [every 4 rows] 29 (30, 30, 31) times, incorporating new sts into cable pattern—112 (118, 124, 130) sts.

Work even until piece measures approx 18 (18, 19½, 19½) inches, ending on Chart Row 12 or 24. Bind off.

Finishing

Weave in yarn tails. Wet block the pieces to finished measurements.

Sew shoulder seams.

Button Band

With RS facing and using smaller needle, pick up and knit approx 174 (186, 198, 210) sts along left front, making sure that you have a multiple of 4 sts + 2.

Row 1 (WS): *P2, k2; rep from * to last 2 sts, p2.

Row 2: *K2, p2; rep from * to last 2 sts, p2.

Work even in rib for 5 rows.

Bind off loosely in rib.

Place markers for 6 evenly spaced buttons along band, making the first button ½ inch from top and the last 5 inches from the lower edge.

Buttonhole Band

Work as for button band until 3 rows rib are complete.

Next row: Work eyelet buttonholes [yo, k2tog] opposite the markers.

Work even in rib for 4 rows.

Bind off loosely in rib.

Collar

With RS facing and using smaller needles, pick up and knit 94 (94, 114, 114) sts along the neckline.

Row 1 (WS): *K2, p2; rep from * to last 2 sts, k2.

Row 2: *P2, k2; rep from * to last 2 sts, p2.

Work even for 5 rows.

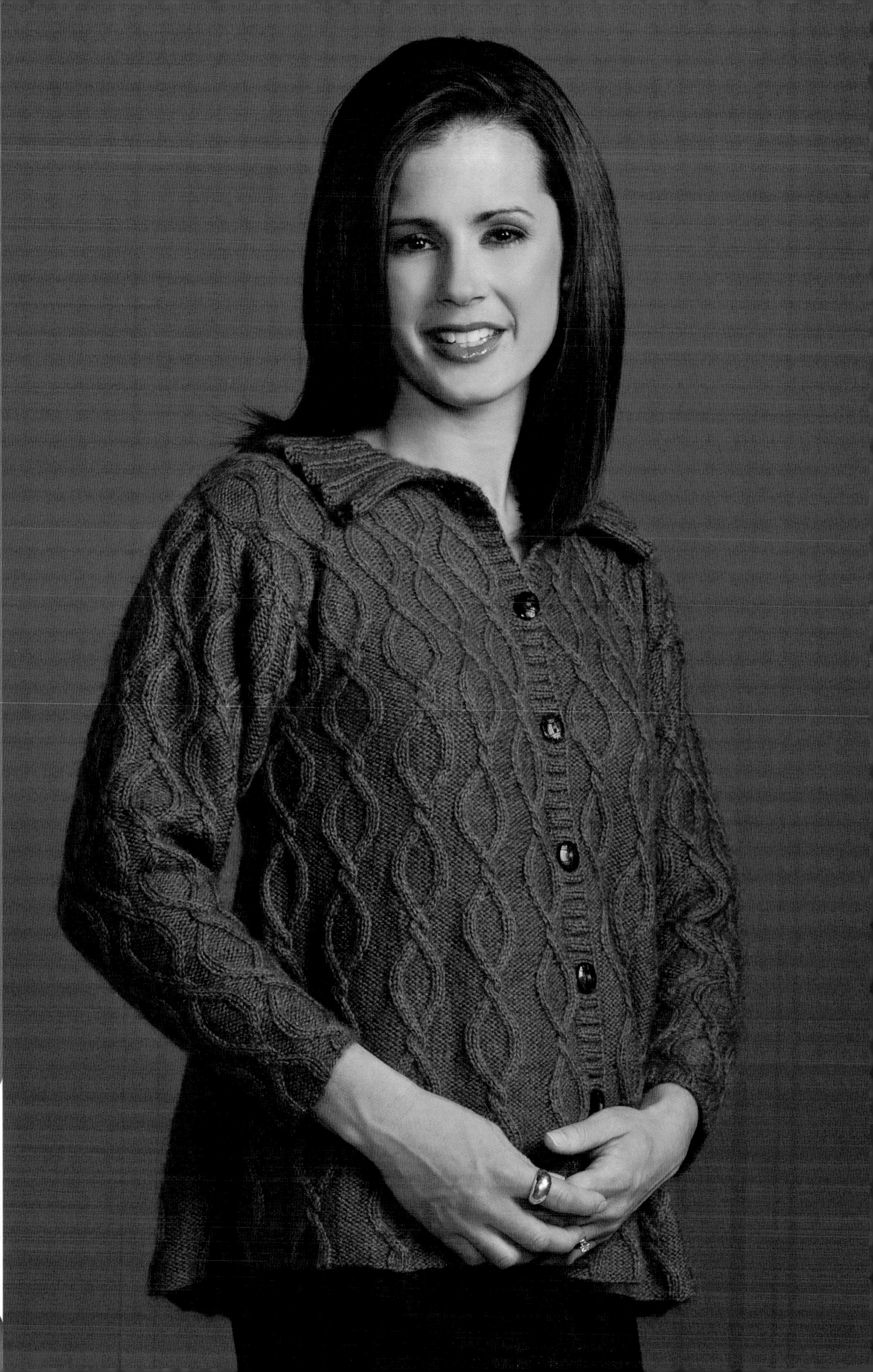

Inc row (RS): *P2, L1-R, k2; rep from * to last 2 sts, p2.

Next row: *K2, p3; rep from * to last 2 sts, k2.

Work even for 6 rows.

Inc row (RS): *P2, L1-R, k3; rep from * to last 2 sts, p2.

Next row: *K2, p4; rep from * to last 2 sts, k2.

Work even for 6 rows.

Inc row: *P2, L1-R, k4; rep from * to last 2 sts, p2.

Next row: *K2, p5; rep from * to last 2 sts, k2.

Work even for 6 rows.

Bind off loosely.

Assembly

Measure approx 8½ (9, 9½, 10) inches down from shoulders and place marker for sleeve position. Sew sleeves between markers. Sew side and sleeve seams. Weave in tails. ■

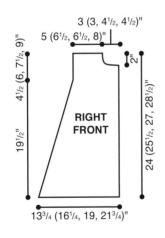

RIGHT FRONT

3 (3, 4½, 4½)"

5 (6½, 6½, 8)"

4½ (6, 7½, 9)"

2"

19½"

24 (25½, 27, 28½)"

13¾ (16¼, 19, 21¾)"

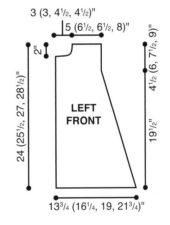

LEFT FRONT

3 (3, 4½, 4½)"

5 (6½, 6½, 8)"

4½ (6, 7½, 9)"

2"

19½"

24 (25½, 27, 28½)"

13¾ (16¼, 19, 21¾)"

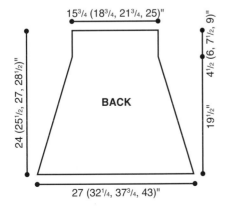

BACK

15¾ (18¾, 21¾, 25)"

4½ (6, 7½, 9)"

19½"

24 (25½, 27, 28½)"

27 (32¼, 37¾, 43)"

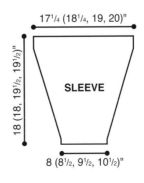

SLEEVE

17¼ (18¼, 19, 20)"

18 (18, 19½, 19½)"

8 (8½, 9½, 10½)"

Double-Zip Cardigan

Design by Leslye Solomon

Enjoy knitting this updated, figure-flattering classic of an asymmetrical jacket.

Materials

Brown Sheep Shepherd's Shades (heavy worsted weight; 100% wool; 131 yds/100g per skein): 8 (10, 11) skeins pearl #SS110

Size 8 (5mm) needles

Size 10 (6mm) needles or size needed to obtain gauge

Size J/10 (6mm) crochet hook

Stitch holder

2 separating zippers

Straight pins

Sewing thread to match zipper

Sewing needle

Thimble

Small pearl buttons (optional)

Skill Level

 INTERMEDIATE

Sizes

Woman's small/medium (large/extra-large, 2X/3X-large) Instructions are given for smallest size, with larger sizes in parentheses. When only 1 number is given, it applies to all sizes.

Finished Measurements

Chest: 39 (48, 57) inches

Length to shoulders: 22 (22½, 23) inches

Gauge

16 sts and 22 rows = 4 inches/10cm in St st with larger needles.

22 sts and 22 rows = 4 inches/10cm in K2, P2 Rib (slightly stretched) with smaller needles.

21 sts and 22 rows = 4 inches/10cm over cable pat (panel and purl sts combined) with larger needles.

To save time, take time to check gauge.

Special Abbreviations

2 over 2 Right Cross (2/2 RC): Sl 2 to cn and hold to back; k2, k2 from cn.

Make 1 Purlwise (M1-p): Insert LH needle from front to back under the running thread between the last st worked and next st on RH needle; purl into the back of resulting loop.

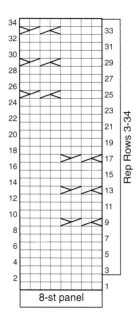

CABLE PANEL

Pattern Stitch

Cable Panel (8-st panel)

Row 1 and all non-cabled RS rows: K8.

Row 2 and all WS rows: P8.

Rows 9, 13 and 17: 2/2 RC, k4.

Rows 25, 29 and 33: K4, 2/2 RC.

Row 34: P8.

Rep Rows 3-34 for pat.

Pattern Notes

Because of the elasticity of the ribbed fabric, each of the sizes will fit a wide range of bodies.

Length of armholes will seem short because the saddle shoulder section of the sleeve will add length when assembled.

If desired, work mirrored-cable patterns on each front. To do this, on left front, work Rows 1 and 2 of cable chart, then skip to Row 19 and continue from there. You can mirror the cable pattern on the left and right sleeves as well.

If you prefer a longer length, an additional skein of yarn is needed.

All shaping decreases are worked right at the edge.

Tassel and inner zipper embellishments are optional.

Back

With smaller needles, cast on 98 (122, 146) sts.

Row 1 (WS): P2, *k2, p2; rep from * to end.

Row 2 (RS): K2, *p2, k2; rep from * to end.

Work even in established rib until piece measures 2 inches, ending with a WS row.

Change to larger needles and begin working cable pat.

Row 1 (RS): P3, *Cable panel over next 8 sts, p4; rep from * to last 11 sts, Cable panel over next 8 sts, p3.

Row 2: K3, *Cable panel, k4; rep from * to last 3 sts, k3.

Work even until piece measures 7½ inches, ending with a WS row.

Bodice shaping

Inc row (RS): P1, M1-p, work to last st, M1-p, p1— 100 (124, 148) sts.

Work even for 20 rows (working new sts in rev St st), then rep Inc row—102 (126, 150) sts.

Work even until piece measures approx 14½ inches or desired length to underarm, ending with a WS row.

Shape armholes

Bind off 5 sts at beg of next 2 (4, 4) rows; 4 sts at beg of next 2 rows; 3 sts at beg of next 2 rows; 2 sts at beg of next 2 rows—74 (88, 112) sts.

Dec 1 st each side [every other row] 2 (5, 4) times— 70 (78, 102) sts.

Work even until armhole measures 8 (8½, 9) inches, ending with a WS row.

Shape shoulders

Loosely bind off 8 (10, 15) sts at beg of next 2 rows, then 9 (10, 16) sts at beg of following 2 rows—36 (38, 40) sts.

Slip rem sts to holder for back of neck.

Right Front

With smaller needles, cast on 37 (49, 61) sts.

Row 1 (WS): P1, *k2, p2; rep from * to end.

Row 2 (RS): *K2, p2; rep from * to last st, k1.

Work even in established rib until piece measures 2 inches, ending with a WS row.

Change to larger needles and begin working cable pat.

Row 1 (RS): P2, *Cable panel over next 8 sts, p4; rep from * to last 11 sts, Cable panel over next 8 sts, p3.

Row 2: K3, *Cable panel, k4; rep from * to last 10 sts, Cable panel, p2.

Work even until piece measures 7½ inches, ending with a WS row.

Bodice shaping

Inc row (RS): Work to last st, M1-p, p1—38 (50, 62) sts.

Work even for 20 rows (working new st in rev St st), then rep Inc row—39 (51, 63) sts.

Work even until piece measures same as back to underarm, ending with a RS row.

Shape armhole

At armhole edge, bind off 5 sts 1 (2, 2) time(s); 4 sts once; 3 sts once and 2 sts once—25 (32, 44) sts.

Dec 1 st at armhole edge [every other row] 2 (5, 4) times—23 (27, 40) sts.

Work even until armhole measures 6 (6½, 7) inches, ending with a WS row.

Shape front neck

Bind off 2 (3, 5) sts at neck edge once—21 (24, 35) sts.

Dec 1 st at neck edge [every RS row] 4 times—17 (20, 31) sts.

Work even until armhole measures same as for back, ending with a RS row.

Shape shoulder

At armhole edge, loosely bind off 8 (10, 15) sts once, then 9 (10, 16) sts once.

Left Front

With smaller needles, cast on 37 (49, 61) sts.

Row 1 (WS): *P2, k2; rep from * to last st, p1.

Row 2 (RS): K1, *p2, k1; rep from * to end.

Work even in established rib until piece measures 2 inches, ending with a WS row.

Change to larger needles and begin working cable pat.

Row 1 (RS): P2, *Cable panel over next 8 sts, p4; rep from * to last 11 sts, Cable panel over next 8 sts, p3.

Row 2: K3, *Cable panel, k4; rep from * to last 10 sts, Cable panel, p2.

Work even until piece measures 7½ inches, ending with a WS row.

Bodice shaping

Inc row (RS): P1, M1-p, work to end—38 (50, 62) sts.

Work even for 20 rows (working new st in rev St st), then rep Inc row—39 (51, 63) sts.

Work even until piece measures same as back to underarm, ending with a WS row.

Shape armhole

At armhole edge, bind off 5 sts 1 (2, 2) time(s); 4 sts once; 3 sts once, and 2 sts once—25 (32, 44) sts.

Dec 1 st at armhole edge [every other row] 2 (5, 4) times—23 (27, 40) sts.

Work even until armhole measures 6 (6½, 7) inches, ending with a RS row.

Shape front neck

Bind off 2 (3, 5) sts at neck edge once—21 (24, 35) sts.

Dec 1 st at neck edge [every WS row] 4 times—17 (20, 31) sts.

Work even until armhole measures same as for back, ending with a WS row.

Shape shoulder

At armhole edge, loosely bind off 8 (10, 15) sts once, then 9 (10, 16) sts once.

Sleeves

With smaller needles, cast on 42 (42, 46) sts.

Row 1 (WS): P2, *k2, p2; rep from * to end.

Row 2 (RS): K2, *p2, k2; rep from * to end.

Work even in established rib until piece measures 2½ inches.

Change to larger needles.

Row 1 (RS): K2, p15 (15, 17), work Cable panel over next 8 sts, p15 (15, 17), k2.

Row 2: P2, k15 (15, 17), Cable panel, p8, k15 (15, 17), p2.

Work 4 rows even in established pat.

Inc row (RS): K2, M1-p, work in established pat to last 2 sts, M1-p, k2—44 (44, 48) sts.

Maintaining pat, rep Inc row [every 6 rows] 10 (10, 12) times, working new sts in rev St st—64 (64, 72) sts.

Work even until sleeve measures 18 inches (or desired length), ending with a WS row.

Sleeve cap

Bind off 4 sts at beg of next 2 rows—56 (56, 64) sts.

Dec 1 st each side [every other row] 14 times—28 (28, 36) sts.

Bind off 3 (3, 4) sts at beg of next 6 (6, 4) rows, then 0 (0, 5) sts at beg of next 0 (0, 2) rows—10 sts.

Saddle shoulder

Work even for approx 3¼ (3¾, 6) inches or until saddle measures same as shoulders.

Place sts on holder.

Finishing

Weave in ends. Block pieces to finished measurements.

Sew saddle shoulder of sleeve to bound-off shoulders of back and the two fronts.

Sew sleeve caps into armholes.

Collar

With RS facing and smaller needle, beg at right neck edge, pick up and knit/work as follows: along right front neck edge to saddle: pick up and knit 11 sts; across saddle: k2tog, k6, k2tog; across back neck: k1 in each knit st and [k2tog] twice across each set of 4 purl sts; across saddle: work as for previous saddle; along left front neck: pick up and knit 11 sts. Count your sts. On next row, adjust (inc or dec) if necessary so that total number of collar sts is a multiple of 4 sts plus 2.

Row 1 (WS): P2, *k2, p2; rep from * to end.

Row 2 (RS): K2, *p2, k2; rep from * to end.

Work even in established rib until collar measures 3 inches or desired length.

With larger needle, bind off very loosely in rib.

Center Panel

With smaller needles, cast on 22 (26, 26) sts.

Row 1 (WS): P2, *k2, p2; rep from * to end.

Row 2 (RS): K2, *p2, k2; rep from * to end.

Work even until piece measures same as front to top of collar.

Weave in ends.

Block center panel.

Sew sleeve and side seams.

Install Zippers

Using crochet hook, work sc in every other row along the right front edge (avoid crocheting too tightly; the edge should lie flat). Without turning, ch 1, and work backwards sc, page 81 (crab st) in each sc. Fasten off.

Rep along left front edge and both edges of center panel.

Baste zipper in place using a sewing needle and thread, allowing the extra length of the zipper to extend above the neck. Position the crochet edge so the teeth of the zipper are covered.

Backstitch or machine-sew (using a zipper foot) through the line between the single crochet and the rev sc sts. Move the zipper pull down. Sew the thread zipper stoppers on both sides of the zipper slightly below where the zipper will be trimmed. Trim the zipper above the zipper stopper.

Weave in all ends. Steam if necessary.

Tassels (optional)

Cut 5 strands of yarn 6 inches long. Pull ends through hole in zipper pull so that there are 3 inches each side. Wrap another strand of yarn several times around all strands, then cut and secure the ends. Unravel the

3 plies of each strand of yarn so that tassel is fluffy. Trim to desired length.

Rep for other zipper.

Inner zipper embellishment (optional)

To make back side of zipper interesting when cardigan is unzipped, embellish as desired. As pictured, sew small pearl buttons to zipper tape, or embroider, sew beads or do whatever your imagination dictates. ∎

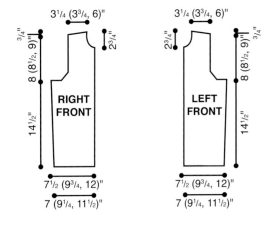

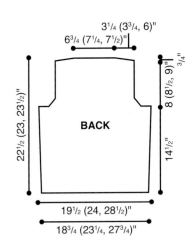

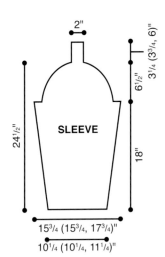

Serene

Design by Jean Clement

This stylish tunic with honeycomb eyelets and form-fitting details is sure to complement your wardrobe.

Materials

Mission Falls 136 Merino Superwash (DK weight; 100% superwash merino wool; 136 yds/50g per ball): 10 (11, 13, 14, 15) balls putty #015

Size 4 (3.5mm) 16- and 29-inch circular needles

Size 7 (4.5mm) 16- and 29-inch (or longer) circular needles or size needed to obtain gauge

Stitch markers (1 in CC for beg of rnd)

Spare needle for 3-needle bind-off

Skill Level

■■■■ EXPERIENCED

Sizes

Woman's extra-small (small, medium, large, extra-large) Instructions are given for smallest size, with larger sizes in parentheses. If only 1 number is given, it applies to all sizes.

Finished Measurements

Chest: 30 (33, 37¾, 40¼, 45¼) inches

Length: 28½ (29, 29½, 29½, 30) inches

Gauge

21 sts and 28 rnds/rows = 4 inches/10cm in St st with larger needle.

24 sts and 32 rnds/rows = 4 inches/10cm in Honeycomb Eyelet pat with larger needle.

To save time, take time to check gauge.

Note: Work swatches both flat and in the round, because gauge may change and you may need to use a different needle size for each.

Special Abbreviations

Place marker (pm): Place a marker on needle to separate sections.

Slip, slip, slip, knit (sssk): Slip next 3 sts one at a time kwise, then knit these 3 sts tog tbl.

Lifted Increase Right (L1-R): K1 in st 1 row below next st.

Lifted Increase Left (L1-L): K1 in st 2 rows below last st worked.

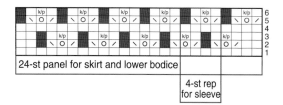

24-st panel for skirt and lower bodice

4-st rep for sleeve

HONEYCOMB EYELET

STITCH KEY
☐ K on RS, p on WS
◹ K2tog on RS, p2tog on WS
○ Yo
◺ Ssk on RS, ssp on WS
k/p K1, p1 in same st
■ No stitch

Pattern Stitches

Honeycomb Eyelet (24-st panel)

Note: *St count decreases on Rnds 2 and 5, returning to original count on Rnds 3 and 6.*

Rnd 1: K24.

Rnd 2: K2, *k2tog, yo, ssk; rep from * 4 times, k2—19 sts.

Rnd 3: K3, *(k1, p1) into the yo of previous rnd, k2; rep from * 4 times, k1—24 sts.

Rnd 4: K24.

Rnd 5: *K2tog, yo, ssk; rep from * 5 times—18 sts.

Rnd 6: K1, *(k1, p1) into the yo of previous rnd, k2; rep from * 5 times, k1—24 sts.

Rep Rnds 1-6 for pat.

Honeycomb Eyelet (for sleeves; multiple of 4 sts)

Note: *St count decreases on Rnds 2 and 5, returning to original count on Rnds 3 and 6.*

On Rnd 3, keep beg of rnd consistent by moving marker between [k1, p1 into yo of previous rnd]. First k2tog of Rnd 5 will include the p1 st that will not have been knit in Rnd 4.

Rnd 1: Knit.

Rnd 2: *Ssk, k2tog, yo; rep from * to end.

Rnd 3: *K2, (k1, p1) into yo of previous rnd; rep from * to end.

Rnd 4: Knit.

Rnd 5: *K2tog, yo, ssk; rep from * to end.

Rnd 6: K1, *(k1, p1) into yo of previous rnd, k2; rep from * ending last rep k1.

Rep Rnds 1-6 for pat.

Pattern Notes

This garment is worked in the round in 1 piece from the bottom to the armholes, after which back and fronts are worked back and forth. The ribbed waist is intended to sit approx 1½ inches above the natural waistline. The sleeves are picked up from the armhole and worked in the round to the cuff; the cap is formed using short rows.

It will be helpful to place markers on either side of each Honeycomb Eyelet Panel.

Optional bust shaping is given.

Read the Short Row chapter before working short rows. All short rows can be worked with knitter's preferred technique to prevent a hole at the turn on each end of a short row.

Sweater

With larger 29-inch needle, cast on 200 (224, 256, 280, 312) sts; pm for beg of rnd and join, taking care not to twist sts.

Rnds 1 and 2: K1, p2, *k2, p2; rep from * to last st, k1.

Pat set-up rnd: *[K7 (10, 14, 17, 21), pm, work Rnd 1 of Honeycomb Eyelet Panel over next 24 sts, pm] 3 times, k7 (10, 14, 17, 21), pm for side edge; rep from * once.

Work even in established pats until piece measures 14 inches or to desired length, ending with Rnd 6 of Honeycomb Eyelet Panel.

Ribbed waist

Next rnd: Change to smaller needle; knit around, removing all markers except side and beg of rnd markers.

Dec rnd (extra-small only): *P1, k2, [p2tog, k2] 9 times, [p2, k2] 6 times, [p2tog, k2] 9 times, p1; rep from * once more—164 sts.

Dec rnd (all other sizes): K1, p2tog, [k2, p2tog] 10 (12, 14, 16) times, [k2, p2] 6 times, [k2, p2tog] 22 (26,

30, 34) times, [k2, p2] 6 times, [k2, p2tog] 11 (13, 15, 17) times, k1—180 (204, 220, 244) sts.

Next 10 rnds: Work even in established rib; rib should measure approx 1½ inches.

Bodice

Next rnd: Change to larger needle; knit around.

Set-up rnd: *K29 (33, 39, 43, 49), pm, work Rnd 1 of Honeycomb Eyelet Panel over next 24 sts, pm, k29 (33, 39, 43, 49); rep from * once.

Work even until bodice measures approx 2½ inches above ribbing, ending with Rnd 6 of Honeycomb Eyelet Panel.

Bust shaping (optional)

Bust shaping is worked in short rows across the front only. Directions for working short rows are given in The Art of Short Rows, page 106.

Maintaining established pat, work as follows:

Row 1 (RS): Knit to 3 (5, 7, 8, 10) sts before side marker, turn.

Row 2 (WS): Purl to 3 (5, 7, 8, 10) sts before beg of rnd marker, turn.

Row 3: Knit to 6 (10, 14, 16, 20) sts before side marker, turn.

Row 4: Purl to 6 (10, 14, 16, 20) sts before beg of rnd marker, turn.

Row 5: Knit to 9 (15, 21, 24, 30) sts before side marker, turn.

Row 6: Purl to 9 (15, 21, 24, 30) sts before beg of rnd marker, turn.

Next rnd (RS): Working in the round, k41 (45, 51, 55, 61), L1-L, L1-R, k82 (90, 102, 110, 122) [joining short rows as you come to them if you've worked optional bust shaping], L1-L, L1-R, k41 (45, 51, 55, 61)—168 (184, 208, 224, 248) sts.

Cut yarn.

Bodice and neckline shaping

Work remainder of bodice back and forth. Leave beg of rnd marker in place to mark second side of tunic.

Notes: The front eyelet panels will move toward the shoulders using decs that also shape the neckline.

On the back, incs and decs are used to angle the eyelet panels outward toward the shoulders; this will not affect the st counts.

Slip first 42 (46, 52, 56, 62) sts to RH needle, rejoin yarn between center front sts with WS facing.

Row 1 (WS): P1 (neck-edge st), *p2tog, ssp, yo; rep from * once, p2tog, p2, pm, p58 (66, 78, 86, 98) joining short rows as you come to them, *ssp, yo, p2tog; rep from * twice, pm, p2, pm, *ssp, yo, p2tog; rep from * twice, p58 (66, 78, 86, 98), pm, p2, *ssp, yo, p2tog; rep from * once, ssp, p1 (neck edge st)—156 (172, 196, 212, 236) sts.

Row 2 (RS): K1, *k2, (k1, p1) into yo of previous row; rep from * once, k61 (69, 81, 89, 101), *k1, (k1, p1) into the yo of previous row, k1; rep from * twice, k2, *k1, (k1, p1) into the yo of previous row, k1; rep from * twice, k61 (69, 81, 89, 101), *(k1, p1) into the yo of previous row, k2; rep from * once, k1—166 (182, 206, 222, 246) sts.

Row 3: Purl.

Row 4 (shaping row): K1, *k2tog, yo, ssk; rep from * once, k2tog, yo, sssk, k56 (64, 76, 84, 96), k3tog, *yo, ssk, k2tog; rep from * once, yo, ssk, L1-L, k2, L1-R, *k2tog, yo, ssk; rep from * once, k2tog, yo, sssk, k56 (64, 76, 84, 96), k3tog, *yo, ssk, k2tog; rep from * once, yo, ssk, k1—154 (170, 194, 210, 234) sts.

Row 5: P1,*p1, (k1, p1) into yo of previous row, p1; rep from * twice, p56 (64, 76, 84, 96), *p1, (k1, p1) into yo of previous row, p1; rep from * twice, p4, *p1, (k1, p1) into yo of previous row, p1; rep from * twice,

p56 (64, 76, 84, 96), *p1, (k1, p1) into yo of previous row, p1; rep from * twice, p1—164 (180, 204, 220, 244) sts.

Row 6: Knit.

Work 6 rows in pats as established, shaping neck on front and moving back eyelet panels out on Row 4 (new sts between back panels are worked in St st).

Divide fronts and back

Next row (RS): *Work in established pat to 5 (5, 7, 7, 8) sts past marker, sl 10 (10, 14, 14, 16) sts just worked to waste yarn for underarm; rep from * once, work in established pat to end of row. Place right front and back sts on another piece of waste yarn.

Note: Work armhole shaping on fronts and back as follows: At beg of row: K1, ssk, continue in pat; at end of row: Work to last 3 sts, k2tog, k1.

Fronts

Work each front separately, continuing neckline shaping as established.

Right front

Beg with a WS row and continuing established pat, dec 1 st at armhole edge [every RS row] twice, then [every other RS row] 0 (4, 6, 10, 12) times—23 (23, 24, 24, 26) sts.

Work even until armhole measures 8½ (8½, 9, 9, 9½) inches, ending with a WS row.

Shape shoulder

Shoulders are shaped using short rows; maintain Honeycomb Eyelet pat as much as possible.

Row 1 (RS): Work 14 (14, 16, 16, 16) sts, turn.

Row 2: Sl 1, work 13 (13, 15, 15, 15) sts, turn.

Row 3: Work 7 (7, 8, 8, 8) sts, turn.

Row 4: Sl 1, work 6 (6, 7, 7, 7) sts, turn.

Row 5: Work across all sts, closing short rows as you come to them.

Place sts on waste yarn.

Left front

Work as for left front to shoulder shaping, ending with a RS row.

Shape shoulder

Row 1 (WS): Work 14 (14, 16, 16, 16) sts, turn.

Row 2: Sl 1, work 13 (13, 15, 15, 15) sts, turn.

Row 3: Work 7 (7, 8, 8, 8) sts, turn.

Row 4: Sl 1, work 6 (6, 7, 7, 7) sts, turn.

Row 5: Work across all sts, closing short rows as you come to them.

Place sts on waste yarn.

Back

With WS facing, sl 84 (92, 104, 112, 124) back sts to larger needle and join yarn.

Row 1 (WS): Work WS row in established pat.

Row 2 (RS): Maintaining pat, dec 1 st at armhole edge [every RS row] 0 (2, 2, 4, 7) times, then [every other RS row] 0 (1, 2, 3, 3) times—74 (76, 82, 84, 88) sts.

Work even until armhole measures 8½ (8½, 9, 9, 9½) inches, ending with a RS row.

Shape shoulders

Shoulders are shaped using short rows; maintain Honeycomb Eyelet pat as much as possible.

Next row (WS): Work across, turn.

Next row: Work 23 (23, 24, 24, 26) sts, turn.

Next row: Sl 1, work 12 (12, 12, 12, 13) sts, turn.

Next row: Sl 1, work 53 (55, 59, 61, 63) sts, closing short rows as you come to them, turn.

Next row: Sl 1, work 12 (12, 12, 12, 13) sts, turn.

Next row: Sl 1, work 23 (23, 24, 24, 26) sts, closing short rows as you come to them, turn.

Next row: Purl all sts, closing short rows as you come to them.

Join shoulders

Place right front sts on spare needle; with WS facing, join right front to right side of back using 3-needle bind-off (page 29).

Bind off 28 (30, 34, 36, 36) center-back sts.

Place left front sts on spare needle; with WS facing, join left front to left side of back using 3-needle bind-off.

Sleeves

Pick-up rnd: With larger 16-inch needle, and beg at center underarm, sl 5 (5, 7, 7, 8) held sts onto needle, pick up and knit 39 (39, 43, 43, 50) sts evenly spaced between underarm and shoulder seam, pm, pick up and knit 39 (39, 43, 43, 50) sts evenly spaced between shoulder seam and held sts, knit 5 (5, 7, 7, 8) held underarm sts onto needle, pm for beg of rnd—88 (88, 100, 100, 116) sts.

Shape cap

Row 1 (RS): Knit 13 (13, 15, 15, 15) sts past shoulder marker, turn.

Row 2: Sl 1, purl 13 (13, 15, 15, 15) sts past shoulder marker, turn.

Row 3: Sl 1, knit 15 (15, 17, 17, 17) sts past shoulder marker, closing gap on previous row when you come to it, turn.

Row 4: Sl 1, purl 15 (15, 17, 17, 17) sts past shoulder marker, closing gap on previous row when you come to it, turn.

Continue in this manner, working 2 sts more than the previous row on each pass until all 78 (78, 86, 86, 100) picked-up sts have been worked (do not work underarm sts), ending with a WS row, turn.

Next row (RS): Knit to underarm marker, closing rem gaps as you come to them.

Begin working in the round.

Knit 5 rnds.

Dec rnd: K1, k2tog, knit to 3 sts before end of rnd, ssk, k1—86 (86, 98, 98, 114) sts.

Continue in St st and rep Dec rnd [every 5 rnds] 7 times—72 (72, 84, 84, 100) sts.

Knit 5 rnds.

Next 10 rnds: Change to smaller needle; *k2, p2; rep from * around.

Change to larger 16-inch needle; work Honeycomb Eyelet pat until sleeve measures 17½ (17½, 17½, 18,

18) inches from underarm (or desired length), ending with Rnd 6 of pat.

Next rnd: Knit.

Next 2 rnds: *K2, p2; rep from * around.

Bind off.

Neckline trim

Rnd 1: With smaller 29-inch needle, beg at right shoulder, pick up and knit 28 (30, 34, 36, 36) sts across back neck, 1 st at shoulder seam, 63 (64, 66, 67, 67) sts evenly spaced along left front, pm, 63 (64, 66, 67, 67) sts evenly spaced along right front, 1 st at shoulder seam, pm for beg of rnd—156 (160, 168, 172, 172) sts.

Rnd 2: *P2, k2; rep from * around.

Rnd 3: *P2, k2; rep from * to 3 sts before center front marker, p1, k2tog, slip marker; ssk, p1, k2; *p2, k2; rep from * to end of rnd.

Rnd 4: Rep Rnd 3.

Bind off, maintaining decs as established at center front.

Weave in all ends.

Block to finished measurements. ∎

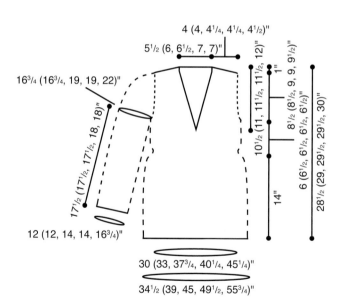

Casual Cabled Hoodie

Design by Amy Polcyn

This seamless, fun-to-knit design is the perfect pullover for a casual weekend.

Materials

- Mission Falls 1824 Wool (100% superwash wool; worsted weight; 85 yds/50g per ball): 16 (18, 20, 22, 23) balls pistachio #028
- Size 8 (5mm) double-point, 16-inch, 24-inch and 32-inch circular needles or size needed to obtain gauge
- Spare 16-inch circular needle
- Stitch markers, 1 in CC for beg of rnd
- Stitch holders
- Cable needle

Skill Level

 INTERMEDIATE

Sizes

Woman's small (medium, large, extra-large, 2X-large) Instructions are given for smallest size, with larger sizes in parentheses. When only 1 number is given, it applies to all sizes.

Finished Measurements

Chest: 35½ (39½, 43½, 47½, 51½) inches

Length: 26½ (27¾, 28¾, 30¼, 31½) inches

Gauge

18 sts and 24 rnds = 4 inches/10cm in St st.

Cable panel = 2½ inches/6cm wide.

To save time, take time to check gauge.

Special Abbreviations

Place marker (pm): Place a marker on needle to separate sections.

Knit in front and back of stitch (kfb): Inc by knitting in front loop, then in back loop of st.

Wrap and Turn (W&T): Turn for short row, using desired method of eliminating hole at turn. (see The Art of Short Rows, page 106)

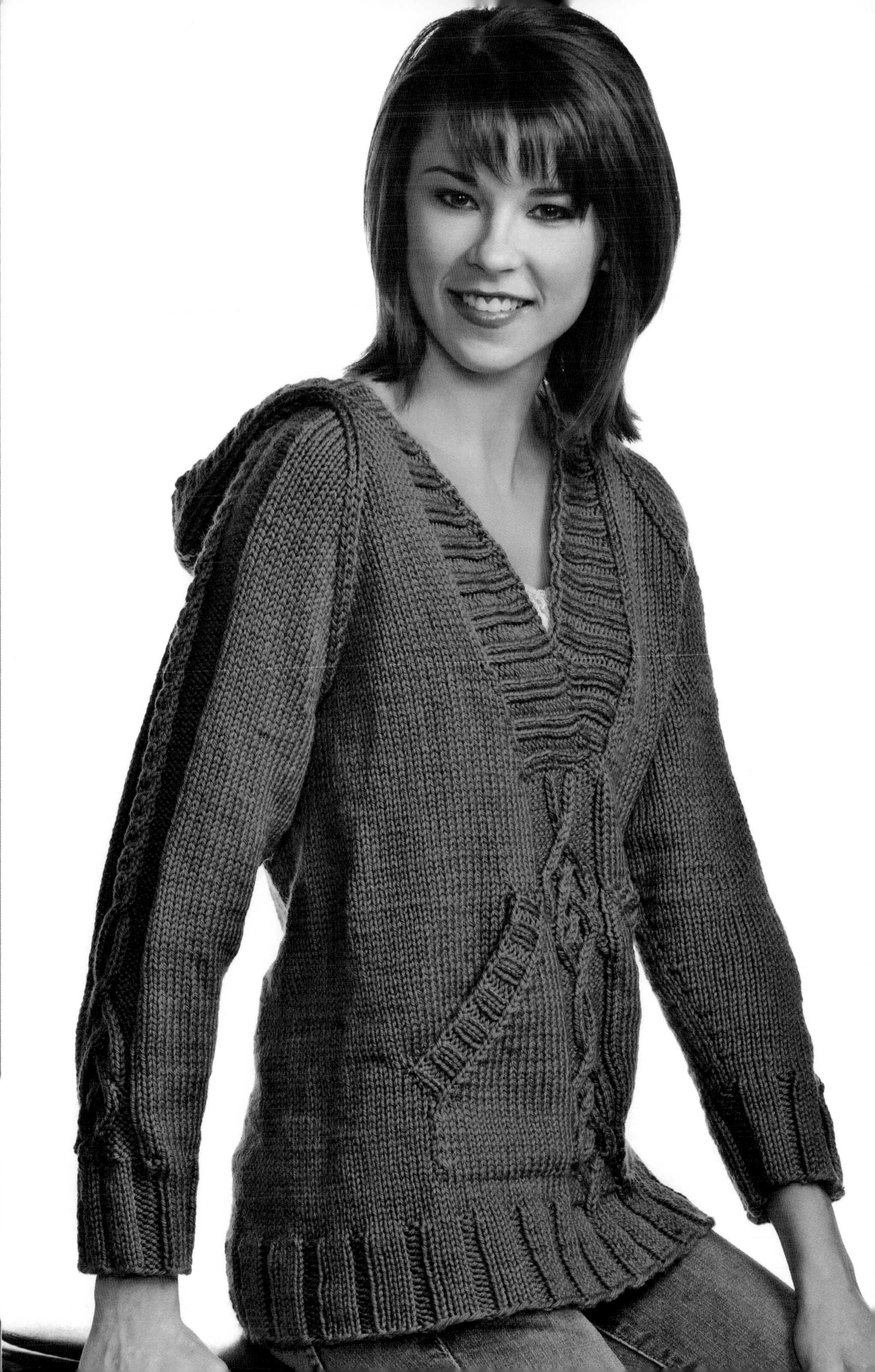

Special Techniques

3-needle bind-off: With RS tog and needles parallel, using a 3rd needle, knit tog a st from the front needle with 1 from the back. *Knit tog a st from the front and back needles, and slip the first st over the 2nd to bind off. Rep from * across, then fasten off last st.

Short rows: See Short Row chapter.

Pattern Stitch

Cable Panel (20-st panel)

For front, rep Rnds 1-36 for pat.

For sleeves, work Rnds 1-40 once, then rep Rnds 37-40 only to end.

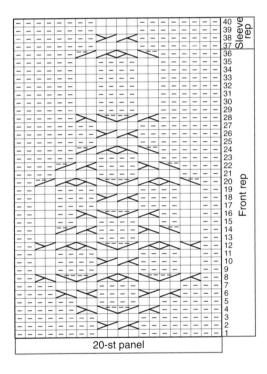

CABLE PANEL

STITCH KEY
☐ K on RS, p on WS
⊟ P on RS, k on WS
⤬ Sl 2 to cn and hold in back; k2, k2 from cn
⤬ Sl 2 to cn and hold in back; k2, p2 from cn
⤬ Sl 2 to cn and hold in front; p2, k2 from cn
⤬ Sl 2 to cn and hold in front; k2, k2 from cn
Note: For Front, rep Rnds 1-36. For Sleeve, work Rnds 1-40, rep Rnds 37-40

Pattern Notes

Body and sleeves are worked separately in the round to underarms after which they are joined to work the yoke seamlessly to end.

The front has more stitches than the back to account for cable panel.

Neck edging is worked using short rows. Read Short Row chapter and used desired method.

When working sleeve, change to 16-inch circular needle when there are enough stitches to do so.

When working the yoke, change to shorter circular needle as desired.

If desired, slip first sleeve to a spare circular needle (same size or smaller than main needle) to keep stitches on hold.

Body

With longer circular needle, cast on 168 (186, 204, 222, 240) sts; pm for beg of rnd and join, taking care not to twist sts.

Work in K4, P2 Rib for 3 inches and on last rnd, work 88 (96, 106, 114, 124) sts for front, pm for "side seam", work 80 (90, 98, 108, 116) sts for back to end of rnd.

Cable set-up rnd: K34 (38, 43, 47, 52), pm, work Rnd 1 of Cable Panel over next 20 sts, pm, knit to end of rnd.

Work even in established St st and Cable Panel until piece measures 4 (4½, 5, 5½, 6) inches.

Divide for pocket

Next rnd: K14 (16, 19, 21, 24), work center front 60 (64, 68, 72, 76) sts and place on 16-inch circular needle to hold for pocket flap, knit to end.

Next rnd: Work to held sts, cast on 60 (64, 68, 72, 76) sts over gap (behind held sts), knit to end.

Work in St st until piece measures 12 (12½, 13, 13½, 14) inches.

Set aside.

Pocket flap

Working pocket flap sts back and forth in rows, cast on 1 selvage st at each side on first row, then work even for 2 inches, maintaining established Cable

Panel and ending with a WS row—62 (66, 70, 74, 78) sts.

Dec row (RS): K1, ssk, work to last 3 sts, k2tog, k1—60 (64, 68, 72, 76) sts.

Rep Dec row [every RS row] 17 times—26 (30, 34, 38, 42) sts.

Work even until flap measures 8 inches, ending with a RS row and on last row, work k2tog at beg of row and ssk at end of row to eliminate selvage sts—24 (28, 32, 36, 40) sts.

Cut yarn, leaving a 6-inch tail.

Join flap and body

Next rnd: K32 (34, 37, 39, 42) front sts; holding pocket flap sts in front of main body sts, *work 1 st of flap tog with 1 st of body; rep from * until all flap sts are worked, maintaining Cable Panel pat; knit to end of rnd.

Work even until body measures 13½ (14, 14½, 15, 15½) inches

Divide for neck

Next rnd: Knit to marker, bind off 20 Cable Panel sts, knit past beg of rnd marker (now side marker), continuing to bound-off sts—148 (166, 184, 202, 220) sts.

Work 3 rows even in St st.

Neck dec row (RS): K1, ssk, knit to last 3 sts, k2tog, k1—146 (164, 182, 200, 218) sts.

Rep Neck dec row [every 4 rows] 4 times, working last neck decs while working yoke.

When neck measures 3 inches, ending after a WS row, divide for armholes as follows:

Next row (RS): *Knit to 4 sts past side marker, slip last 8 sts worked to holder for underarm; rep from * once, knit to end.

Set body aside.

Sleeves

With dpns, cast on 48 (48, 48, 60, 60) sts; pm for beg of rnd and join, taking care not to twist sts.

Rib set-up rnd: *[P2, k4] 2 (2, 2, 3, 3) times, p2*, pm; [p2, k4] 3 times, p2, pm; rep from * to * once more.

Continue in established rib until piece measures 3 inches.

Cable set-up rnd: Work in St st to marker, work Rnd 1 of Cable Panel to next marker, knit to end.

Work 2 rnds maintaining established pat.

Inc rnd: Kfb, work to last 2 sts, kfb, k1—50 (50, 50, 62, 62) sts.

Rep Inc rnd [every 4 rnds] 0 (0, 5, 0, 0) times, then [every 6 rnds] 8 (13, 10, 7, 13) times, then [every 8 rnds] 3 (0, 0, 5, 1) times—72 (76, 80, 86, 90) sts.

Work even until sleeve measures 16½ (17, 17½, 18, 18½) inches, ending with an odd-number rnd and on last rnd, stop 4 sts before beg of rnd marker.

Place 8 underarm sts (4 sts on each side of marker) on a holder—64 (68, 72, 78, 82) sts rem on needle.

Cut yarn, leaving a 10-inch tail; set sleeve aside, using spare needle if desired.

Yoke

Reminder: *Complete front neck decs while working yoke.*

Row 1 (RS): With RS of body facing and beg at right front neck, work to underarm, pm; work in pat across 64 (68, 72, 78, 82) right sleeve sts, pm; k72 (82, 90, 100, 108) back sts, pm; work in pat across left sleeve sts, pm; work left front sts.

Work 1 WS row even.

Raglan dec row (RS): *Work to 2 sts before marker, k2tog, slip marker, ssk; rep from * 3 times, knit to end—8 sts dec.

Rep Raglan dec row [every RS row] 23 (25, 26, 28, 30) times, omitting decreases on fronts when 3 sts rem on each, ending with a WS row—62 (68, 78, 88, 92) sts.

Hood

Work 12 rows even (maintaining rem Cable Panel sts from sleeves) and on last row, work 31 (34, 39, 44, 46) sts, pm for center back hood, work to end.

Inc row (RS): Work to 2 sts before marker, kfb, k1, slip marker, kfb, work to end—64 (70, 80, 90, 94) sts.

Rep Inc row [every 4 rows] 13 times—90 (96, 106, 116, 120) sts.

Work even until hood measures 13 inches, ending with a WS row.

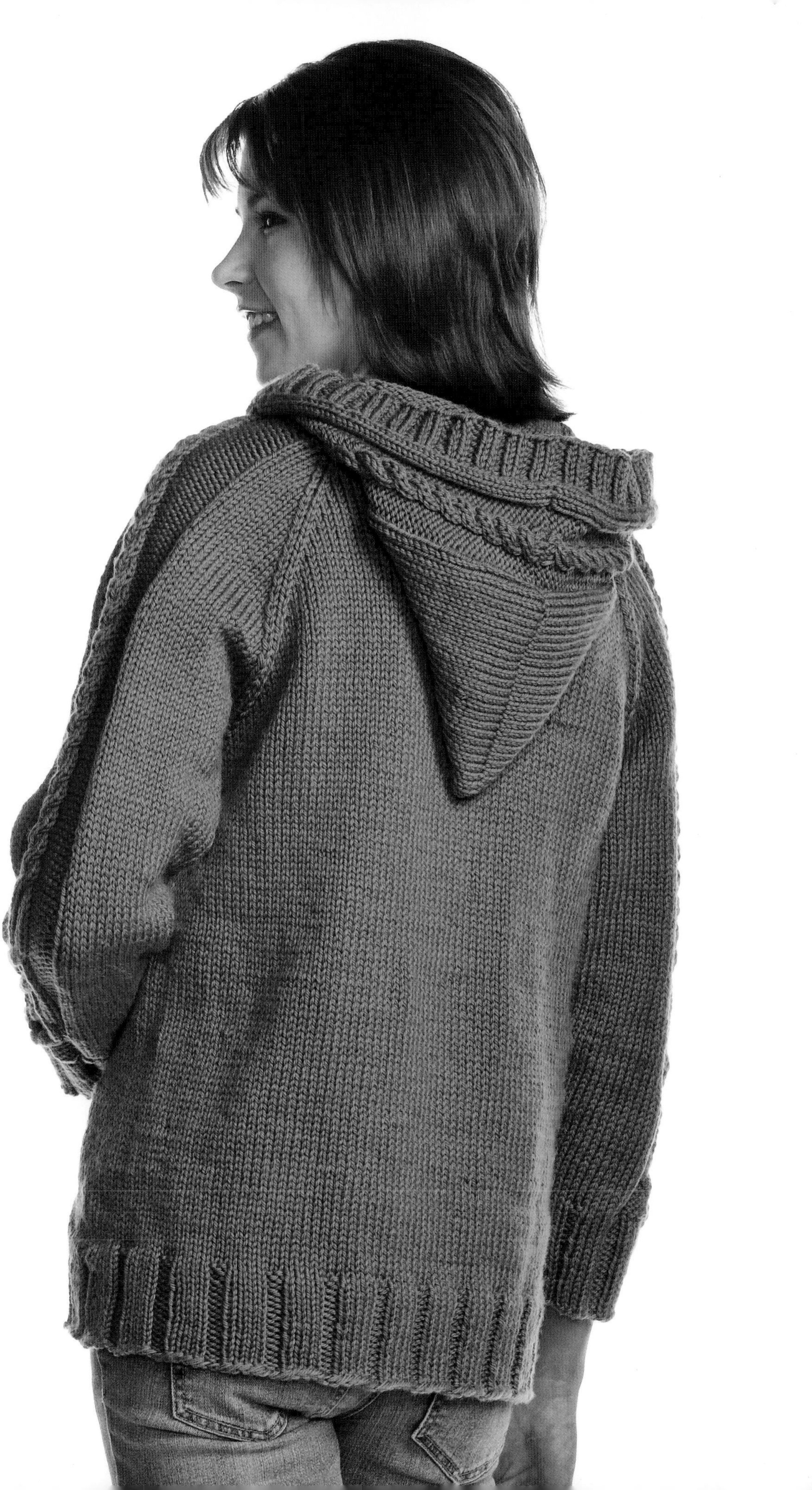

Fold hood in half with RS tog; close top seam with 3-needle bind-off.

Finishing

With RS facing, beg at right front neck edge, pick up and knit 198 (206, 214, 222, 230) sts along front neck and hood edges, leaving bound-off center neck sts open.

Row 1 (WS): P2, *k2, p2; rep from * to end.

Work 4 more rows in established rib and on last row, pm on each side at point where hood meets the front.

**Next 2 rows (short rows): Work in pat to 3 sts before first marker, W&T; work in pat to end.

Next 2 rows (short rows): Work in pat to 3 sts before wrapped st, W&T; work in pat to end.

Rep [last 2 rows] 4 times.**

Next row (RS): Work across entire row, hiding wraps as you come to them.

Rep from ** to **.

Bind off all sts loosely in rib, hiding wraps as you come to them.

Overlap left front edge with right front edge and sew to bound-off edge of front cable panel, going through all 3 layers.

Pocket Trim

With RS facing, pick up and knit 26 sts along angled edge of pocket.

Row 1 (WS): P2, *k2, p2; rep from * to end.

Work 4 more rows in established rib.

Bind off loosely in rib.

Rep on other side of pocket.

Using mattress stitch, sew bottom 2 inches of pocket flap and side edges of rib trim to body.

Sew open bottom edge of body to pocket.

Graft underarms with Kitchener stitch (page 42).

Weave in ends. Block to finished measurements. ■

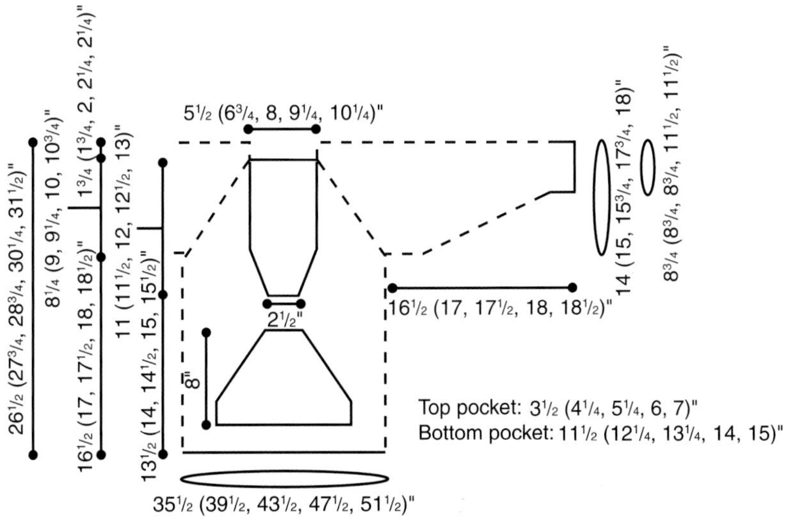
5½ (6¾, 8, 9¼, 10¼)"
26½ (27¾, 28¾, 30¼, 31½)"
8¼ (9, 9¼, 10, 10¾)"
1¾ (1¾, 2, 2¼, 2¼)"
16½ (17, 17½, 18, 18½)"
11 (11½, 12, 12½, 13)"
13½ (14, 14½, 15, 15½)"
2½"
8"
16½ (17, 17½, 18, 18½)"
14 (15, 15¾, 17¾, 18)"
8¾ (8¾, 8¾, 11½, 11½)"
Top pocket: 3½ (4¼, 5¼, 6, 7)"
Bottom pocket: 11½ (12¼, 13¾, 14, 15)"
35½ (39½, 43½, 47½, 51½)"

Caring for Your Finished Garment by Jodi Lewanda

After completing your perfect project, you should take special care laundering and storing it.

Review the yarn label to determine how to wash your garment. The label(s) will instruct you to hand-wash, machine-wash or professionally dry clean your garment.

If the yarn label is unavailable and you have yarn remaining, make a swatch and hand-wash it in lukewarm (not hot or cold) water and your soap of choice. Be careful not to pick a soap that has bleach or fabric softener additives. Do not agitate your swatch. Make sure to note any changes in shape, either stretching or shrinking. Be especially aware of any changes in swatches that use more than one yarn (even different colors of the same yarn) because they may react differently.

Once you have determined your method of laundering, handle your project carefully. The soap you use should be well mixed in the water before you submerge the project; the water should cover the project completely. Gently work the soapy water through your garment. After your piece is clean, squeeze out any excess water, then rinse thoroughly until all soap is removed.

Place your garment between two clean, absorbent towels and gently squeeze out any remaining water. Lay your project flat to dry, easing it into shape and keeping it away from direct sunlight and heat.

Once the project is totally dry, you should fold it carefully to store it. Do not put your finished garment on a hanger because it will stretch out.

Dirt and dust are enemies of hand knits. Closed containers, sweater bags, sweater boxes or zippered cases are better storage solutions than open shelving. Sealed containers also deter mildew and help keep out moths.

Final Thoughts

If you take the time to follow these simple steps to ensure the long life of your beautifully knitted garments, you will enjoy wearing them for many years to come.

General Information

Basic Stitches

Garter Stitch

When working back and forth, knit every row. When working in the round on circular or double-point needles, knit one round, and then purl one round.

Stockinette Stitch

When working back and forth, knit right-side rows and purl wrong-side rows. When working in the round on circular or double-point needles, knit all rounds.

Reverse Stockinette Stitch

When working back and forth, purl right-side rows and knit wrong-side rows. When working in the round on circular or double-point needles, purl all rounds.

Ribbing

Ribbing combines knit and purl stitches within a row to give stretch to the garment. Ribbing is most often used for cuffs of hats or socks, but may be used for the entire piece.

The rib pattern is established on the first row. On subsequent rows, the knit stitches are knitted and purl stitches are purled to form the ribs.

Reading Pattern Instructions

Before beginning a pattern, read through it to make sure you are familiar with the abbreviations that are used.

Some patterns may be written for more than one size. In this case, the smallest size is given first and others are placed in parentheses. When only one number is given, it applies to all sizes.

You may wish to highlight the numbers for the size you are making before beginning. It is also helpful to place a self-adhesive sheet on the pattern to note any changes made while working the pattern.

Measuring

To measure pieces, lay them flat on a smooth surface. Take the measurement in the middle of the piece, not along the outer edge where the edges tend to curve or roll.

Working From Charts

Charts are provided both for more complicated stitch patterns as well as color work. On the chart each square represents one stitch. A key is given indicating the color or stitch represented by each color or symbol in the box.

The row number is always given at the side of the chart that the row begins. If the number is at the right (usually right-side, odd-numbered rows), read right to left; if it is at the left (usually wrong-side, even-numbered rows), read left to right.

For color-work charts, rows beginning at the right represent the right side of the work and are usually knit. Rows beginning at the left represent the wrong side and are usually purled.

When working in rounds, every row on the chart is a right-side row, and is read from right to left.

Use of Zero

In patterns that include various sizes, zeros are sometimes necessary. For example, k0 (0, 1) means if you are making the smallest or middle size, you would do nothing, and if you are making the largest size, you would k1.

Glossary

bind off—used to finish an edge

cast on—process of making foundation stitches used in knitting

decrease—means of reducing the number of stitches in a row

increase—means of adding to the number of stitches in a row

intarsia—method of knitting a multicolored pattern into the fabric

knitwise—insert needle into stitch as if to knit

make 1—method of increasing using the strand between the last stitch worked and the next stitch

place marker—placing a purchased marker or loop of contrasting yarn onto the needle for ease in working a pattern repeat

purlwise—insert needle into stitch as if to purl

right side—side of garment or piece that will be seen when worn

selvage (selvedge) stitch—edge stitch used to make seaming easier

slip, slip, knit—method of making a left-leaning decrease by moving stitches from left needle to right needle and working them together

slip stitch—an unworked stitch slipped from left needle to right needle, usually as if to purl

wrong side—side that will be inside when garment is worn

work even—continue to work in the pattern as established without working any increases or decreases

work in pattern as established—continue to work following the pattern stitch as it has been set up or established on the needle, working any increases or decreases in such a way that the established pattern remains the same

yarn over—method of increasing by wrapping the yarn over the right needle without working a stitch

Standard Abbreviations

[ ] work instructions within brackets as many times as directed

( ) work instructions within parentheses in the place directed

** repeat instructions between the asterisks as directed

* repeat instructions following the single asterisk as directed

" inch(es)

approx approximately

beg begin/begins/beginning

CC contrasting color

ch chain stitch

cm centimeter(s)

cn cable needle

dec decrease/decreases/decreasing

dpn(s) double-point needle(s)

g gram(s)

hdc: half double crochet

inc increase/increases/increasing

k knit

k2tog knit 2 stitches together

kwise knitwise

LH left hand

m meter(s)

M1 make one stitch

MC main color

mm millimeter(s)

oz ounce(s)

p purl

pat(s) pattern(s)

p2tog purl 2 stitches together

psso pass slipped stitch over

pwise purlwise

rem remain/remains/remaining

rep repeat(s)

rev St st reverse stockinette stitch

RH right hand

rnd(s) round(s)

RS right side

sc single crochet

skp slip 1 stitch knitwise, k1, pass slipped stitch ove—one stitch decreased

sk2p slip 1 knitwise, knit 2 together, pass slipped stitch over the knit 2 together—2 stitches have been decreased

sl slip

sl 1 kwise slip 1 knitwise

sl 1 pwise slip 1 purlwise

sl st slip stitch(es)

ssk slip 2 sts 1 at a time knitwise, then knit them together—a left-leaning decrease.

ssp slip 2 sts 1 at a time knitwise, then purl them together through the back loops—a left-leaning decrease

st(s) stitch(es)

St st stockinette stitch/stocking stitch

tbl through back loop(s)

tog together

WS wrong side

wyib with yarn in back

wyif with yarn in front

yd(s) yard(s)

yfwd yarn forward

yo yarn over

Skill Levels

BEGINNER

Projects for first-time knitters using basic knit and purl stitches. Minimal shaping.

EASY

Projects using basic stitches, repetitive stitch patterns, simple color changes and simple shaping and finishing.

INTERMEDIATE

Projects with a variety of stitches (such as basic cables and lace) simple intarsia, double-point needles and knitting-in-the-round techniques, mid-level shaping and finishing.

EXPERIENCED

Projects using advanced techniques and stitches, such as short rows, Fair Isle, more intricate intarsia, cables, lace patterns and numerous color changes.

Metric Conversion Chart

INCHES INTO MILLIMETRES & CENTIMETRES (Rounded off slightly)

inches	mm	cm	inches	cm	inches	cm	inches	cm
1/8	3	0.3	5	12.5	21	53.5	38	96.5
1/4	6	0.6	5 1/2	14	22	56	39	99
3/8	10	1	6	15	23	58.5	40	101.5
1/2	13	1.3	7	18	24	61	41	104
5/8	15	1.5	8	20.5	25	63.5	42	106.5
3/4	20	2	9	23	26	66	43	109
7/8	22	2.2	10	25.5	27	68.5	44	112
1	25	2.5	11	28	28	71	45	114.5
1 1/4	32	3.2	12	30.5	29	73.5	46	117
1 1/2	38	3.8	13	33	30	76	47	119.5
1 3/4	45	4.5	14	35.5	31	79	48	122
2	50	5	15	38	32	81.5	49	124.5
2 1/2	65	6.5	16	40.5	33	84	50	127
3	75	7.5	17	43	34	86.5		
3 1/2	90	9	18	46	35	89		
4	100	10	19	48.5	36	91.5		
4 1/2	115	11.5	20	51	37	94		

KNITTING NEEDLES CONVERSION CHART

Canada/U.S.	0	1	2	3	4	5	6	7	8	9	10	10½	11	13	15
Metric (mm)	2	2¼	2¾	3¼	3½	3¾	4	4½	5	5½	6	6½	8	9	10

Standard Yarn Weight System

Categories of yarn, gauge ranges, and recommended needle sizes

Yarn Weight Symbol & Category Names	1 SUPER FINE	2 FINE	3 LIGHT	4 MEDIUM	5 BULKY	6 SUPER BULKY
Type of Yarns in Category	Sock, Fingering, Baby	Sport, Baby	DK, Light Worsted	Worsted, Afghan, Aran	Chunky, Craft, Rug	Bulky, Roving
Knit Gauge* Ranges in Stockinette Stitch to 4 inches	27–32 sts	23–26 sts	21–24 sts	16–20 sts	12–15 sts	6–11 sts
Recommended Needle in Metric Size Range	2.25–3.25mm	3.25–3.75mm	3.75–4.5mm	4.5–5.5mm	5.5–8mm	8mm and larger
Recommended Needle U.S. Size Range	1 to 3	3 to 5	5 to 7	7 to 9	9 to 11	11 and larger

* GUIDELINES ONLY: The above reflect the most commonly used gauges and needle sizes for specific yarn categories.

Knitting Basics

Knit (K)

With yarn in back, insert tip of right needle from front to back in next stitch on left needle.

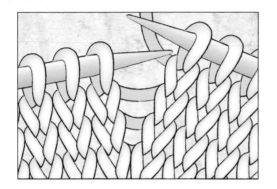

Bring yarn counterclockwise around the tip of the right needle.

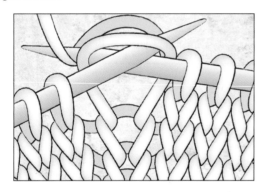

Pull yarn loop through the stitch with right needle point.

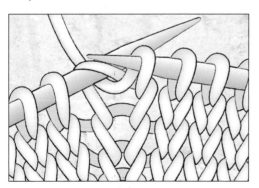

Slide the stitch off the left needle. The new stitch is on the right needle.

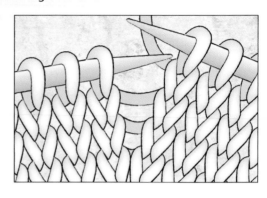

Purl (P)

With yarn in front, insert tip of right needle from back to front through front loop of the next stitch on the left needle.

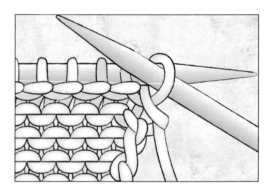

Bring yarn around the right needle counterclockwise.

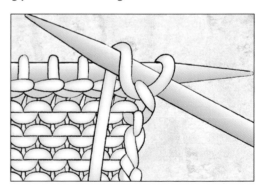

With right needle, draw yarn back through the stitch.

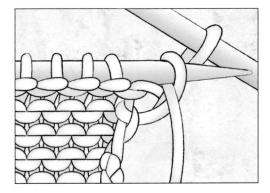

Slide the stitch off the left needle. The new stitch is on the right needle.

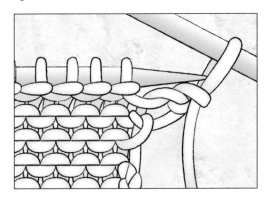

Increase (inc)

Two stitches in one stitch
Increase (knit)

Knit the next stitch in the usual manner, but don't remove the stitch from the left needle.

Place right needle behind left needle and knit again into the back of the same stitch. Slip original stitch off left needle.

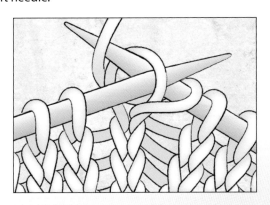

Increase (purl)

Purl the next stitch in the usual manner, but don't remove the stitch from the left needle.

Place right needle behind left needle and purl again into the back of the same stitch. Slip original stitch off left needle.

Make 1 Increase (M1)

Invisible Increase

Insert left needle from front to back under the horizontal loop between the last stitch worked and next stitch on left needle.

With right needle, knit into the back of this loop.

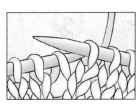

Backward Loop Increase over the right needle

With your thumb, make a loop over the right needle.

Slip the loop from your thumb onto the needle and pull to tighten.

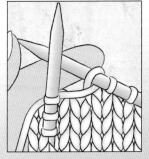

Increase in top of stitch below

Insert tip of right needle into the stitch on left needle one row below.

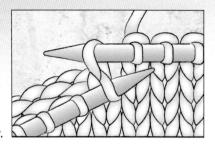

Knit this stitch, and then knit the stitch on the left needle.

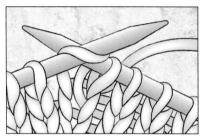

Slip, Slip, Knit (ssk)

Slip next two stitches, one at a time as if to knit, from left needle to right needle.

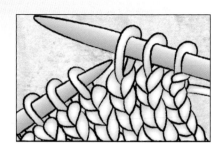

Insert left needle in front of both stitches and knit them together as one.

Decrease (Dec)

Knit 2 together (k2tog)

Put tip of right needle through next two stitches on left needle as to knit. Knit these two stitches as one.

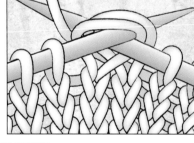

Purl 2 together (p2tog)

Put tip of right needle through next two stitches on left needle as to purl. Purl these two stitches as one.

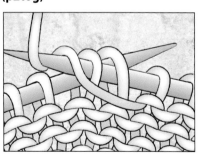

Slip, Slip, Purl (ssp)

Slip next two stitches, one at a time as if to knit, from left needle to right needle. Slip these stitches back onto left needle keeping them twisted.

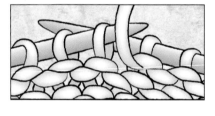

Purl these two stitches together through back loops.

Crochet Basics

Some knit items are finished with a crochet trim or edging. Below are some abbreviations used in crochet and a review of some basic crochet stitches.

Chain Stitch (ch)

Begin by making a slip knot on the hook. Bring the yarn over the hook from back to front and draw through the loop on the hook.

For each additional chain stitch, bring the yarn over the hook from back to front and draw through the loop on the hook.

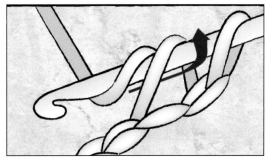

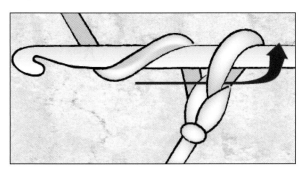

Half Double Crochet (hdc)

Yo, insert hook in st, yo, pull through st, yo, pull through all 3 lps on hook.

Single Crochet (sc)

Insert the hook in the second chain through the center of the V. Bring the yarn over the hook from back to front.

Draw the yarn through the chain stitch and onto the hook.

Again bring yarn over the hook from back to front and draw it through both loops on hook.

For additional rows of single crochet, insert the hook under both loops of the previous stitch instead of through the center of the V as when working into the chain stitch.

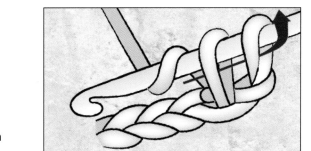

Slip Stitch (sl st)

Insert hook under both loops of the stitch, bring yarn over the hook from back to front and draw it through the stitch and the loop on the hook.

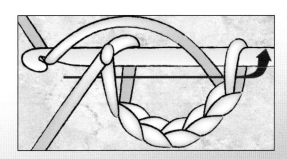

Working in the Round
Working With Double-Point Needles
Helpful Tips:

Make sure that the cast on edge remains along the inside of the circle on each needle. This will help prevent the stitches from twisting around the needles.

Slip the first cast-on stitch from the left-hand needle tip to the right-hand needle tip. Slip the last cast-on stitch from the right-hand needle tip up and over the stitch just transferred and onto the left-hand needle tip to "join" into a ring.

4 Double-Point Needles

Cast on the number of stitches required. Distribute the stitches as instructed in the pattern on 3 double-point needles. Position the needles so that needle 1 is on the left and needle 3 is on the right. The yarn you're about to work with should be attached to the last stitch on needle 3.

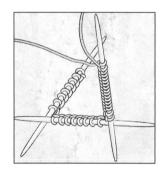

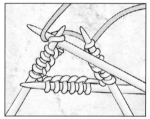

5 Double-Point Needles

Cast on the number of stitches required. Distribute stitches evenly on 4 double-point needles.

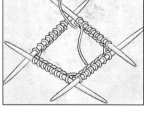

Position the needles so that needle 1 is on the left and needle 4 is on the right. The yarn you're about to work with should be attached to the last stitch on needle 4.

Matching Patterns

When it comes to matching stripes and other elements in a design, a simple formula makes things line up perfectly:

Begin the seam in the usual way.

Enter the first stitch of each new color stripe (or pattern detail) on the same side as you began the seam (i.e. the same side as your tail).

Embroidery Stitches

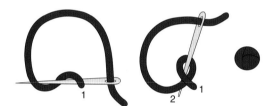

French Knot

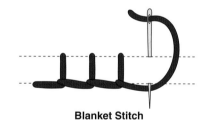

Blanket Stitch

Chain Stitch

Special Thanks

We would like to thank the following designers for their imaginative designs, without which this book would not be possible.

Kate Atherley

Preplanning With Finishing in Mind, 17

Special Cast-On & Bind-Off Method, 22

Construction Essentials: Garment Assembly, Seaming & Weaving Methods, 38

Jean Clement

Fully Fashioned Elements, 99

The Art of Short Rows, 106

Serene, 148

Jennifer Hagan

Blocking Fundamentals, 32

Arenda Holladay

No-Nonsense Neckline & Collar Treatments, 48

The ABCs of Buttonholes, 73

Cable Swing Sweater, 135

Jodi Lewanda

Making the Gauge Swatch, 12

Tailored Elements: Hems & Facings, 64

Decorative Details: Bands, Borders & Ribbing, 88

Caring for Your Finished Garment, 162

Amy Polcyn

Casual Cabled Hoodie, 155

Colleen Smitherman

Creating the Perfect Pocket, 54

Leslye Solomon

The Wonderful World of Working With Zippers, 79

Double-Zip Cardigan, 142

Myra Wood

Enticing Embellishments, 113

Wild Flower Purse, 130

Project Designers

Kate Atherley is a knitter, teacher, designer and writer based in Toronto. Her particular passion is socks, but she also loves lace and cables—anything that's a good challenge! Kate is the technical editor of *Socks for Knitty*, and knitting editor of the Canadian needlecraft magazine *A Needle Pulling Thread*. In addition to being a frequent contributor to *Yarn Forward*, one of the UK's most popular knitting magazines, she's had designs published in a variety of books, including Amy Singer's *No Sheep for You*, Lion Brand's *Just Socks*, and the 2007 Knitting Pattern-A-Day Calendar. See more of her work at www.wisehildaknits.com.

Jean M. Clement Having been born into an artistic family, Jean learned all types of needlework and to look at the world with an artisanal eye at a very young age. Her earliest crafting memory is of sitting on a bed with one of her sisters at an aunt's home in Great Britain and knitting slippers. While the slippers are long gone, the love of crafting—especially knitting—has remained.

With a background in both knitting and sewing/tailoring, Jean likes to design garments that are fashionable while remaining classic—garments that can be worn for years. She also is continuously looking for new techniques to learn and incorporates that new knowledge into her work.

Jean released her first professional knitting pattern in 2005 and has since continued to add to her pattern line—Desert Rose Designs.

When not knitting, thinking about knitting or dreaming up new designs, Jean loves to spend time with her husband of 35 years, her four Italian Greyhounds and one Australian Cattle Dog in the high plains of Colorado where they live.

Jennifer Hagan left a career in education to get back to crafts and now spends her days running two pattern lines for knitting and crochet, Figheadh Yarnworks and Mirth. Jen also does freelance knitting and crochet design and a little local teaching. In all of these endeavors, Jen tries to encourage knitters and crocheters to pay close attention to finishing and especially blocking their work for just the right finish. Originally from Alabama, Jen Hagan now lives in the Pacific Northwest with husband Fred. Most of Jen's family still lives down south. She has three daughters and four grandchildren.

See more of Jen's work at www.jenhagan.com.

Arenda Holladay is an advisor to the Master Hand Knitting Committee of The Knitting Guild Association which certifies Master Knitters. She is a consulting editor to *Cast On* magazine and frequently contributes technical articles and designs.

Jodi Lewanda has had a passion for creativity for as long as she can remember. A textile design graduate from NYC's Fashion Institute of Technology, she is a published hand knitwear designer and freelances as technical editor of knitting patterns. She enjoys teaching technique and project classes at her local yarn store. When not knitting, Jodi is often found with needle and thread in hand, adding textures and stitch work to her projects.

Amy Polcyn has been designing professionally since 2005. Her work appears regularly in major knitting magazines and in yarn company pattern collections. She loves designing projects that are simple to knit with an interesting twist, such as cables, unusual construction or a bit of color work. In addition to designing, Amy works as a technical editor for yarn companies, magazines and independent designers. Prior to casting off her day job for a full-time career in fiber, she worked for 10 years as an elementary teacher in a school for gifted students. Amy lives in suburban Detroit with her husband of 15 years, 10 year-old daughter and 2 wool-loving cats. In her spare time, Amy enjoys belly dancing, long walks and spending as much time as possible with her spinning wheel.

See what else Amy is up to at www.amypolcyn.com.

Colleen Smitherman has found knitting to be a great way to relax, while creating something beautiful and useful at the same time. She initially worked as an RN and later taught nursing and developmental psychology at several universities and carried out research related to infant development and childhood lead poisoning. She retired a few years ago because "work was beginning to cut too deeply into her knitting time." She and her husband now split their time between rural Wisconsin in the summer and the Low Country of South Carolina in the winter. She always knits with binoculars close at hand to watch the beautiful birds that share her parts of the world.

Leslye Solomon is an enthusiastic, energetic and empathetic teacher. Some of her very popular classes are held at Stitches events and other events within the United States and includes hands-on sweater finishing, comprehensible sweater designing and easy-to-learn (or switch to) continental knitting. Leslye has published a number of sweater designs, is a contributing editor for *Knit 'N Style* magazine and has produced numerous instructional videos/DVDs. Following is a list of Leslye's well-photographed, studio-produced videos: *The Hand-Knitter's Guide to Sweater Finishing, The Absolute Best Way To Learn How To Knit, The Hand Knitter's Guide to Buttonholes and Bands* and *The Hand Knitter's Guide to Making Socks.*

Her book entitled, *The Uncomplicated Knitting Machine*, is used by many fashion design institutions and hand and machine knitters all over the world. Although this book is frequently referred to as the "knitting machine bible", many hand-knitters have found it inspirational for creating their own sweater ideas.

Myra Wood is an internationally known fiber and bead artist and designer. She teaches a wide range of classes in beading, embroidery, crochet and knitting, specializing in all things freeform. She's also appeared on a number of episodes of *Knit and Crochet Today, Knitty Gritty* and *Uncommon Threads* for PBS, DIY and HGTV networks. Myra has had her crochet, knit, jewelry and wearable art patterns published in a wide range of books and magazines, and is the author of: *Creative Crochet Lace* and *Crazy Lace*. Myra has been crocheting, sewing and crafting since she was young and enjoys the opportunity to inspire others creatively. She is also the moderator for the International Freeform Guild—with over 2000 members worldwide—and coordinator for its annual national shows. Galleries of her work can be seen at www.myrawood.com

Photo Index

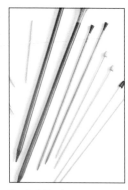